BENJAMIN ROBERTS

First published by Pitch Publishing, 2019

Pitch Publishing
A2 Yeoman Gate
Yeoman Way
Worthing
Sussex
BN13 3QZ
www.pitchpublishing.co.uk
info@pitchpublishing.co.uk

A CIP catalogue record is available for this book
from the British Library.

ISBN 978 1 78531 522 0

Typesetting and origination by Pitch Publishing
Printed and bound in the UK by TJ International, Padstow, Cornwall

Contents

Acknowledgements 7

Introduction 11

I The Brewing & The Session

1. Like Pulling Teeth 19
2. The Battle for Souls 30
3. Down and Out in La Manga and St Etienne . 45
4. A Cup of Plenty 56
5. Mythmaking and Merlot 68

II Saturday Nights and Sunday Mornings

6. Life's a Funny Old Game 83
7. Lead Him to Water 97
8. Just About Managing 113
9. The Wood from the Trees 124
10. Down the Winding Road 136

III The Culture of a Club: Manchester United

11. Irish Spirit, Lancastrian Turf. 169
12. Liquid Assets 191
13. Sink or Swim 200
14. Drinking to Get Drunk 207
15. Fergie Time 219

IV The Recovery

16. Hearts of Gold, Feet of Clay 231
17. Keeping It Simple 250
18. What He Doesn't See 258
19. Last Orders 271

Bibliography 281

ACKNOWLEDGEMENTS

THIS book's journey began around a year ago. After completing *Gunshots & Goalposts*, I gave myself a year off from writing anything new to get married but, a few days after I returned from my honeymoon, *Bottled* was born. This was thanks to my friend Russell Collins, who told me it was time to get writing again while we watched Brighton v Tottenham at a housewarming party. So, thank you – I think – Russell.

A few months later I had settled on a firm idea and I approached Pitch Publishing. After a meeting with Paul in a restaurant where the power cut out at least half a dozen times while we ate, we agreed on a plan to release this book. Here my thanks must go to Paul and Jane Camillin and the rest of the team at Pitch Publishing.

During the writing of this book, I have received help from several people in various practical ways. Harry Robinson, of the *United Through Time* podcast, was an invaluable source on Manchester United's earliest years and their move to Old Trafford. Dimitri Sophos is another. He is not a football fan but happened to be staying at Ashburnham Place when I was working on part of this book and I shared several meals with him between bouts of writing. Alan Gernon is a fellow Pitch Publishing author who has generously shared his knowledge and several contacts with me. Jon Mackenzie is, more than any other, a person without whom this book would probably not exist. He patiently went through my first drafts, told me to remove several hundred semi-colons and gave many helpful suggestions about tone and structure. Cole Moreton should also receive my thanks for his advice on the publishing process and some of the granular details of getting a book published. Thank you Harry, Dimitri, Alan, Cole and Jon.

Several people were interviewed for this book. I would like to thank Shellie Heather and Colin Bland of the Sporting Chance clinic for spending time with me in the tearooms at Champneys. My great thanks also goes to Alan Knight for giving me a few hours of his time. Lorna McClelland was also of great help in providing background which contributed to this book. My thanks go to each of you.

Closer to home, I would like to thank Connor Cross for his practical help and for our shared train journeys. Likewise, Sue and Jennie Oliver for patiently asking me what progress I had made every time you saw me. Paul Burlison and Laura Hagley have provided me with lifts and a place to stay at various points in time. Like all of these people, Steve Oliver has also been a constant source of encouragement. One more Oliver – Pam – convinced me on Christmas Day that this book would benefit from having a picture section. Thank you everyone.

My own parents, Dave and Sharon Roberts, have provided me with a bed at various points in this process when an early train journey was required. My dad, in particular, has also been a useful sounding board during the early months of putting this book together. Similarly, my brother Joel Nicholson-Roberts has provided practical assistance, particularly relating to academic sources. Lastly, and keeping it in the family, my granny Anna Roberts is my biggest cheerleader. My unending appreciation extends to you all.

Finally, and most importantly, to my wife Beth Oliver. She has put up with my almost daily disappearing acts to work on this book and done so with unfailing grace and patience. Thank you for helping me find the stability in life to create projects like this.

Ben Roberts
28 April 2019

INTRODUCTION:
OPENING HOURS

THE books I enjoy reading tend to be those that, while being about football, are about something else too. My first book, *Gunshots and Goalposts*, is as much a look at (Northern) Ireland and its history as it is a sporting tome. So it is with *Bottled*; an examination of how two popular pastimes – drinking and football – have found themselves inextricably linked to one another.

This project partly came about, I suppose, because of my own relationship with alcohol. Quite simply, I cannot drink it safely. Many can, though: humans have been consuming alcohol in its drinkable form since at least 8,000 BC and are still baffled by its (often comical, sometimes tragic) effects. With this in mind, I wanted to understand the particular challenges that footballers face while recognising that, like you and I, they are mere mortals.

There are, of course, footballers who do not fall under the purview of this book who were nevertheless renowned boozers: Garrincha – part of Brazil's 1958 and 1962 World Cup-winning sides – eventually died from liver disease, while the consumption habits of Diego Maradona are the stuff of legend. Theirs should (and probably have been) the subject of other books. My focus, for the most part, is English footballers, or those who have plied their trade at its clubs. The names of Jimmy Greaves, Tony Adams, George Best or the Pauls Gascoigne and Merson will be familiar to our ears, but their stories, as we will discover, are nothing new.

Steve Bloomer, often said to have been England's greatest pre-war player, was regularly fined for being under the influence when he arrived for training at Derby County. Jimmy Cowan, a half-back for Aston Villa, turned out against Bloomer for Scotland against England in 1898 and is said to have behaved 'erratically' during the match, the cause of great scandal. His own Villa team-mate, the full-back Jimmy Crabtree, was another England international and a reserve that day at Celtic Park. He earned 14 caps for his country but died, aged 36, in 1908 when the effects of his alcohol use caught up with him.

My attention was also drawn to the wider context within which football emerged. When this new game was becoming popularised in the late 19th century, some temperance campaigners regarded the increasingly common practice of employing ex-footballers as landlords to draw in thirsty young men as a 'devious device' akin to the high-kicking dancing girls, which were another method of attracting custom. Yet there were other temperance advocates who saw football as a 'powerful rival to boozing', which for a long time had been 'the only excitement open to working men'. Senior figures in the Liverpudlian police force even gave this new game a cautious welcome, noting that the presence of two large clubs in their jurisdiction seemed to be the cause of a reduction in Saturday afternoon drunkenness. Now men had somewhere else to go other than the pub when their half-day shift had finished.

The places where this drinking took (and takes) place is another thread which weaves its way through the following chapters. Pubs have played a central role in the development of English football, its clubs and the institutions that have shaped it. The Football Association was formed in one; namely, the Freemasons Tavern in London's Covent Garden. That was on 23 October 1863, when 11 clubs, drawn mostly from the alumni of elite educational establishments around London, came together to agree a common code of rules which would govern their emerging sport. Here the practice of 'hacking' – kicking a man in the leg – was deemed unacceptable, precipitating a split from the rugby code. A first experimental game under these new rules took place on 19 December 1863, and after a subsequent official fixture on 9 January 1864 a toast was given: 'success to football, irrespective of class or creed'. A further six meetings (all of which took place at the pub) would follow before the association began to establish its authority. Its Scottish counterpart, by contrast, was founded ten years later in one of Glasgow's dry establishments, the Dewar's Temperance Hotel.

Walk three miles north from the original site where the Freemasons Tavern once traded and you will find the Drayton Arms, near to Arsenal's old Highbury stadium. Back in the day, it was reserved strictly for home fans after matches, entrance only gained by reciting the Arsenal team who won the FA Cup in 1971. Journey another few miles north and you will find where the fields behind the White Hart pub once lay. This was where Tottenham Hotspur made their first home and from which their recently vacated stadium took its name. The earliest incarnation of that stadium had been built when Spurs chairman Bobby Buckle had convinced the Charrington brewery that the regular presence of 5,000 men in the immediate vicinity would be good for business. By the 1960s, Tottenham's players and training staff were still meeting in a back room of the Bell and Hare (now called No.8 Tottenham), across the road from the ground, to go over the previous weekend's game and bond through their informal debriefing session.

This brief stroll through the highways and byways of the boroughs of central and north London alone are just the briefest demonstration that football and booze have depended on one another from the very beginning. Join me as I traverse some more. We might even stop at a few pubs along the way.

Ben Roberts,
East Sussex,
2019

*In cockney rhyming slang, bottle
– 'Bottle and glass' – means arse.
Associated with courage and bravery,
to lose your bottle is to lose your arse.*

I
THE BREWING & THE SESSION

1.

LIKE PULLING TEETH

'If you play for England you don't need to drink wine or beer.' – Sven-Goran Eriksson

'He is accused of being arrogant, unable to cope with the press and a boozer. Sounds like he's got a chance to me.' – George Best on Paul Gascoigne

IT'S easy now to see where it all went wrong: a dimly lit bar with low ceilings, famed for nights of debauchery. A drink called Multiple Screaming Orgasms on the cocktail menu. The England team's hotel was practically next door too, in the Causeway Bay area of Hong Kong. When Terry Venables had told his players to go out and enjoy their last night in the city-state following their pre-Euro 96 tour to the Far East, had he really expected them to head out for a few lemonade shandies?

In an adjoining room to the bar of the China Jump club was the dentist's chair, where participants were instructed to lie back in the seat and open their mouths as tequila, vodka and Drambuie were liberally poured down their gullet. Several of the team's stars, including Teddy Sheringham, Steve McManaman and Paul Gascoigne are said to have partaken. When David Cameron's Conservatives came into government 14 years later, one of the first measures his government introduced was to ban such games and 'equipment' across the United Kingdom in an attempt to address the country's apparent binge-drinking epidemic.

Venables did have the foresight to send a chaperone of sorts along to keep an eye on his rowdy players. The fact that it was Bryan Robson, known for his fondness of a pint or ten and by now one of Venables's team of coaches, suggested that the group would not be adhering to a strict two pints and home for a cocoa regime. When they arrived at the venue, Robson had arranged for a corner to be cordoned off for the visiting party where Gascoigne – marking the night before his 29th birthday – and Robbie Fowler playfully fought. The latter had asked a young woman if she 'came here often', much to the Rangers man's dismay.

Pints splashed over heads and shirts were torn to pieces. Robson was left with just the collar round his neck, an act that necessitated a journalist with the team to purchase him a replacement garment from behind the bar. The obligatory pints flowed, topped up with Flaming Lamborghinis – made up of Sambuca, Kahlúa, Baileys and Blue Curaçao – set alight and then downed in one through a straw. A bowl of punch was also available to the players to thirstily sip from. Robson later wrote of how they went from 'near enough sober to absolutely wrecked' in the space of 20 minutes.

The team met their manager-imposed 2.30am curfew, though several had been tucked up in bed for hours already. David Platt had advised Gary Neville and Nick Barmby, young men of 21 and 22, that this would be 'one to miss', while David Seaman had dozed off watching a repeat of the 1993 FA Cup Final. One man, Tony Adams, would have gone along with bells on but for what he knew it would portend if he did so. McManaman and Fowler had tried to persuade him to come along, but he had resisted, telling them 'When we win, I'll have a drink.'

This was, of course, an era before camera phones. It *could* have been possible for the high jinks of that night to have gone unreported. Perhaps there were many more nights like this, lost in the mists of time. But it would be the events of the following day that brought details of the night's exploits out into the open. Gascoigne was given the morning off to celebrate his being a year older, but it was largely moot anyway since training had been cancelled due to an outbreak of bleary-eyedness among the squad. Gascoigne returned around lunchtime from a nearby, smaller hotel and was found by the rest of the players clutching a bottle of champagne in one hand and a cigar in the other. Venables quietly hinted that he needed to put the brakes on.

The flight back to London Heathrow was scheduled for that evening. When it departed, the players were allowed to monopolise the upper deck of the Cathay Pacific flight in the Marco Polo executive section – partly to confine their boisterousness – a decision greeted with chagrin by a number of the FA suits who instead took the players' seats in standard class. This time it was an FA doctor, John Crane, who was tasked with keeping a watchful eye over the young men. Sat next to Gary and Phil Neville, he fell asleep after a couple of drinks.

As those around him played cards, Paul Gascoigne had fallen asleep. That was until Alan Shearer decided to whack him across the back of his head. Rudely awoken from his slumber, Gascoigne roamed up and down the aisles of the plane, on a mission to identify the culprit as he tossed cushions around the cabin. Suspecting Robbie Fowler, Steve McManaman or Rio Ferdinand might be responsible, he struck their back-of-the-seat TV displays until the picture cut out. A disgruntled FA official emerged from downstairs, alerting them to the fact that the commotion could be heard on the deck below. Gascoigne told him to 'fuck off', expressing in no uncertain terms where he saw the official's place in the footballing food chain as he did so.

Eventually, matters aboard flight CX251 were calmed, at least for as long as it took the plane to reach its destination. There it was met by the police, called to investigate the damage that had been done to the aircraft, which was later estimated to be in the region of £5,000. Because the plane was registered overseas, there would be no criminal charges but the airline did seek financial compensation for the harm done to the interior of its 747.

Within days, the press inevitably got wind of events on board. Gascoigne was the subject of a string of tabloid front pages suggesting he should be jettisoned from the squad, if not for football reasons then because of the example he was setting the nation's children. Meanwhile, Venables's recruits had the rest of the week off before reporting to the Burnham Beeches Hotel.

When they convened in Buckinghamshire a few days later, it was decided they would take 'collective responsibility' for what had taken place on the aircraft days earlier. Exactly what, and to what extent, they were admitting culpability to is another question. Gordon Taylor of the Professional Footballers' Association attempted to deflect at least some of the responsibility away from the players for their actions, declaring that, 'If it's drink, the airline must take some responsibility for giving young kids too much.' In several later retellings, Venables himself would continue to deny that anything had even happened on the plane, at odds with the FA's own press release. Still, at least according to one player, their stay at Burnham Beeches was a relatively dry one.

Venables went on to navigate England to a semi-final exit at their home tournament. A disappointing 1-1 draw with Switzerland in the opening game of the competition (during which an apparently unfit Gascoigne was substituted after an hour) was followed by a 2-0 victory over Scotland, during which the same player scored *that* goal and celebrated by having water sprayed into his mouth by Shearer as Jamie Redknapp and McManaman stood by in mimicry of the dentist's chair incident. In the final group fixture, the Dutch were on the wrong end of an unlikely 4-1 thrashing. Misgivings about the players' behaviour and professionalism gave way to the idea that maybe football *could* be coming home. When the quarter-final against Spain was still tied at 0-0 after 120 minutes, David Seaman and Stuart Pearce emerged as heroes of the resultant penalty shootout. All that remained between England and the final was Berti Vogts's Germany.

When that game remained level after another 120 minutes, penalties would provide the answer once more. England's first five takers – Shearer, Platt, Pearce, Gascoigne and Sheringham – had all put theirs away, and so the nation turned to Gareth Southgate, chosen because he appeared enthusiastic about the spot kick despite only ever having taken one before, which had hit the post. This time, Southgate side-footed his effort with his right boot, low and to the left, as the German goalkeeper, Andreas Kopke, dived to block it with his right hand.

During the tournament, the players had been given two days off and Sheringham, Sol Campbell and Redknapp were photographed coming out of a nightclub in Essex at 2.30am. When asked about it, Venables said, 'The Italian players drink wine every day,' adding, 'these boys have sat in a corner and had a couple of beers.' Although other countries had brought beer with them, it had gone largely untouched by their playing staff. Christophe Dugarry viewed the nightclub story with incredulity: 'I simply cannot believe the England players were in a nightclub,' he said, 'you do these sorts of things afterwards, on your holidays.'

❦

It was a nadir for English footballers' representation in the media. Beyond this, it had happened during a widespread moral panic about the nature of the nation's relationship with the bottle. English football fans were seen to have brought shame to the country, leaving a trail of destruction behind them on away trips. This led some to wonder whether the English – or perhaps the British – had a uniquely ruinous relationship with the bottle.

There is a perception that the British are more reckless, destructive drinkers than their European counterparts but, in terms of consumption, we actually imbibe less – the equivalent of 408 pints a year – than our Portuguese (443), French (429), Irish (418) and German (415) counterparts. This would seem to suggest that the issue is not how much we drink, but the *way* we do it. Our continental European neighbours will spread their drinking out over a whole week and, within that, infrequently throughout each day. Yet we condense the large majority of ours into one or two nights a week, during which we guzzle it down as if our lives depended on it.

The difference, it seems, is between 'wet' and 'dry' cultures. In 'wet' cultures, found around the Mediterranean, people drink little and often. They see no immorality in having a small drink with breakfast and another one with lunch. Drink is everywhere but is consumed sparingly. An Italian might have a limoncello with his first meal of the day and another aperitif at lunch. In 'dry' cultures – the UK, US and the Scandinavian nations of northern Europe – alcohol is compartmentalised, found only in certain locations, and is strictly controlled. To have it outside those confined spaces is mostly seen as abnormal and to be avoided. Drinking beyond the two or three nights a week (during which we become explosive boozehounds) is the cause of many a furrowed brow and sideways look.

Lager, today seen as the favoured drink of the stereotypical lout on tour, was introduced to the United Kingdom in the late 1950s. The most popular brand, Skol – originally brewed in Scotland – was aimed at a younger consumer looking to break away from the drinks of their father. If the 50s had been about its introduction, the next decade set the stage for its popularisation: lager had just one per cent market share in 1961, but in the same year it accounted for 19 per cent of advertising spending.

By the mid-1970s, alcohol consumption in the United Kingdom had reached levels not seen since before the First World War. Per-person consumption nearly doubled in the 25 years after 1950. By 1975, lager accounted for 20 per cent of alcohol sales, and in 1996 it made up more than half of all drinks sold in the UK. During the same period, spirit consumption had doubled and the quantity of wine drunk had trebled. As the austerity of the 1950s had faded, the rapidly growing economy of the next few decades meant that the average person had more disposable income. Though pubs still did a solid trade, off-licences and supermarkets sprang up to capitalise on this. It is perhaps unsurprising, then, that in the two decades up to 1970 convictions for drunkenness rose by 50 per cent.

It was an alarming development. In 1979, the Royal College of Psychiatrists published *Alcohol and Alcoholism*, arguing that the government of the day should aim for the goal of 'per capita alcohol consumption ... not increas[ing] beyond the present level, and [...] by stages brought back to a lower level ...' on the basis that it 'can be asserted that if the average man or woman begins to drink more ... then the number of people who damage themselves by their drinking will also increase.' The aim was to bring about a change of attitudes through tax increases on alcohol products and the setting of safe drinking limits which, at the time, were determined to be 56 units for men: a staggering four pints of beer, or more than one bottle of wine, per day. A unit, for context, is measured as a small glass of wine, a small measure of spirits or half a pint of fairly weak beer.

A German mathematician, Walter Ledermann, had presented a thesis in the late 1950s – which became known as the 'Ledermann curve' – suggesting the amount a country drinks per head of population is closely correlated with the proportion of alcoholics – or 'heavy drinkers', depending on your view – it produces. According to Ledermann, it naturally follows that the way to reduce the number of alcoholics in a given nation is to reduce the amount that the country drinks as a whole. Ledermann's findings indicated that even a small increase in per-person consumption has an outsized effect on the number of alcoholics. When moderate drinkers become a little less moderate, the problems they caused to themselves and others did not increase proportionally but actually quite dramatically.

Within five years, those eye-wateringly high recommended daily maximum limits emerging from the RCP report had been more than cut in half. The numbers had never been determined scientifically in the first place. Instead, they were about drawing a line in the sand where one had not existed before, on the basis that any figure was better than no figure at all. The next decade under Margaret Thatcher continued to see a concentration on tackling consumption per capita, which had risen by a shocking 23 per cent between 1971 and 1981. Activities perceived as being enjoyed by the working class were scapegoated as part of this blunt-instrument strategy. Football hooliganism – which certainly existed – was held up as the motif of a degenerate, feckless horde to justify punitive legislation restricting alcohol sales at football games, but not other sporting events. Alcohol consumption was even restricted on transportation *to* those games.

After 25 July 1985, alcohol could no longer be consumed within sight of a football pitch and the income from corporate boxes of some bigger clubs, notably Tottenham and Manchester United, is said to have fallen by £500,000 in the first season after implementation, which eventually led to a review of the legislation, exempting those well-heeled spectators. Yet attendances at football matches fell ten per cent during the season following implementation of the alcohol ban, which was, at least in part, linked to this perceived vilification.

In 1989 another legislative change – the so-called 'Beer Orders' – made the sweeping changes that rippled throughout the 1990s a near inevitability. The Beer Orders had the effect of restricting the number of pubs a single brewery could own, which meant those firms who held more than 1,000 properties had to sell off their excess. By the time the legislation was revoked in 2003, a profound transformation had already taken place. Breweries had sold off a large number of their branches to satisfy the competition authorities, who reckoned that Allied, Bass and their fellow brewers had a stranglehold on the market which allowed them to dictate which ales were stocked and price their independent competitors out of the market.

As a result, the 1990s saw a boom in what were termed 'youth pubs'. These were chains that would play music, offer generous discounts and market themselves to those in their 20s. It was the crystallising of a process that had seen licensed premises shift from being community hubs to retail outlets. In 1950 pubs were so numerous that the average journey time to one was five minutes. The 1960s witnessed a move towards more amateur football being played on Sundays in England (as Sabbatarian instincts waned) with matches often scheduled to end just as pubs opened so players could complete their exertions then roll in for a few pints. In that same decade, a football match or a race meeting were the fifth most common place to travel to the pub *from*. Since then, the purely sporting role of the pub has declined, save for the fact that, for many without access to the various subscriptions, it is the only way to watch their team on television.

The youth pub paradigm of the 1990s saw the rise of the likes of O'Neill's, Wetherspoons and Yates's across city centres. Though this new liberalised era still forbade the advertising of drunkenness itself, it did allow for 2-for-1 promotions, the use of strong mixers and the utilisation of rave culture within advertisements via bright colours and imagery. Where it had once been five, by the time Southgate fluffed *that* penalty it would take 13 minutes for the average person to reach a pub on foot.

2.

THE BATTLE FOR SOULS

'No one ever gets lost on a straight road' –
Charles Clegg, FA chairman and president

FOOTBALL'S complicated relationship with the bottle had begun more than 120 years earlier as competing interests sought to use the new sport of association football to further their moral or commercial objectives.

The first example of this was the cross-pollination of church and sporting activities. Several decades before the rules of association football were codified, evangelicalism had become widespread across most Christian denominations. Many vicars, curates, deacons or otherwise thought sporting teams could help them attract more working-class people to their congregations. Those clergy who were already sportsmen urged their colleagues to become proficient in this new game of football, which was catching on by the 1870s, carrying 'a Bible in one hand and a football in the other'.

Seeing the human body as the site of sin and something to be fought against, a sport which working-class men participated in such as football was the ideal vehicle to indoctrinate them into proper Christian manliness. The Factory Acts of the mid-1870s meant that these men now had a little more free time on a Saturday afternoon and some senior churchmen were worried that it was not being used wisely.

Indeed, the Bishop of Winchester was extremely distressed to think that potential converts were using their leisure time to drink themselves into a state of 'dissipation, riot and drunkenness'.

He was not alone. Across the board, the churches were sceptical about these extra hours that were now available to working men. One prominent figure of the time railed that 'Our streets are reeking with the abuse of pleasure; our society is rotten with it; our social fabric is crumbling beneath it; our best institutions are being shaken and paralysed by it.' For some establishment figures, football was the answer. This was given voice in a *Times* editorial, which explained: 'When you can at the same time enjoy yourself and feel the consciousness that you are doing a moral action, it is difficult to refrain.'

Consumption of alcohol had reached a peak in the 1870s and there was a keenness to provide men with alternative distractions to chart their path to a Godly life. It was hardly surprising, then, that just a decade later a quarter of clubs in the Birmingham area had a connection to one of the city's churches: teams created specifically as an alternative to the pub in the same way that Barnsley (as Barnsley St Peter's) and Bolton Wanderers – originally formed as Christ Church FC – had been.

Quite often, it was church members who sought to form a team, rather than being a recruitment drive led by the officers. Once they had been established, though, players were usually quick to cut ties with the church that had provided them with the resources to get started. Aston Villa had originated out of a Wesleyan Bible class, while their near-neighbours Wolves were a Church of England school team as St Luke's Blakenhall. In this case the impetus seems to have come from the publican father of one of the players, evidence coming from the schoolmaster's diary, in which he wrote, 'Let boys out earlier on Friday and they had a Football Match.' These were often marriages of convenience rather than outright unanimity of purpose. Nevertheless, the early influence of the church on these clubs often carried residual impacts; there was not a single licensed bar within Villa Park until well after World War Two.

In what was then the hotbed of football, many Lancashire clubs, especially Burnley, recruited Scotsmen for their teams. These same Scots would be regarded as a bad influence. Not only were they being paid to play, but they were getting pissed too and encouraging Englishmen to do the same! A good way of tempting such men down to England's north-west had been to offer them the job of landlord at a pub near to the club's ground, an enticement that was to the chagrin of many in the south-east who wanted the game to retain its amateur origins. Half of the Sunderland team of the 1890s were thought to be employed in such a fashion, and early in that same decade Aston Villa had four players working as pub managers. Given this evidence, it's clear that from its earliest days football had a drink culture, and in 1904 Tottenham's captain, a J.L. Jones, wrote that beer was a 'recognised article of diet' for the professional footballer.

In the latter part of the 19th century, many churches and the temperance organisations that were often attached to them began to see football as, if not an unqualified good, then something they were able to make pragmatic accommodations with. Such officials reasoned that even if men had a drink at a football match, the spectacle before them would slow their consumption. The match was seen as an experience in itself and the drinks you might have there were merely an added benefit.

Still, one clergyman from Yorkshire was not convinced, fuming, 'Football is a fascination of the devil and a twin sister of the drink system.' Though the temperance movement and its friends in the church had generally given their grudging support to sport by the early 20th century, sceptical voices remained. Among them was a C.T. Studd who, in 1908, opined that 'a man cannot attend even a football match without making his way to the refreshment bar. It is at the part nearest the drinking bar that one hears the worst language. Men frequently get half-intoxicated and, in most cases, bad-tempered, and so the good name of sport is taken away, never to return until the drinking booths are abolished … ' In a similar vein, a correspondent in the *Lancashire Evening Post* opined, 'We have heard and read a lot about professionalism being an evil, but I think a greater evil exists in the temptations to drinking which are put in the way of professional footballers.'

One argument against the nascent professionalism becoming apparent was that these rowdy players had ample free time and drank too much, which, in turn, encouraged fans to do likewise. Bob Crompton – an early England international – was, however, sceptical about the idea that football encouraged fans to drink to excess. 'The idea is simply preposterous,' he said. 'What happens during the season? They drop in and have one drink after their work on a Saturday afternoon. Then they go off to watch a match, every one of them invigorated by the open air all the time.'

Clapton Orient's Harry Reason also saw the fuss as unnecessary. 'We aren't abstainers by any means,' he told an interviewer, 'but we find that we can enjoy a quiet chat just as well over that beverage as over any other, and know that it will not have a counter-acting effect on our training.' This was, according to Reason, because footballers 'have something else to live for'. He went on to explain that 'footballers can be and are as good citizens as any other class of men. Our life is not made up of drinking, squandering our hard-earned money and betting.'

That may have been true for some men, but Newcastle's Bill Appleyard was aware of the dangers his profession posed: 'Is the life of a footballer full of temptation? Candidly, I must confess it is.' As Appleyard well knew, fans liked to buy drinks for their favourite players. 'It sounds like egotism on my part, and insanity on the part of the type of individual I speak of, but nevertheless it is true,' he said. Another player, Bolton Wanderers' Albert Shepherd, was only too pleased to oblige the pubs which courted his custom. 'This of course,' he clarified, 'was the idea of attracting people to have a quick sing-song and chat. I have some big friends in the business and I have never hesitated to give them a "look-in".'

John Cameron, who was secretary of the Players' Union (a forerunner to the PFA), did not conceal his concern. Writing in *Spaldings Football Guide*, he suggested, 'The worst temptation the beginner has got to face is that of drink. When you become a popular pet your admirers think that they can best show their appreciation of you by buying you beer and Scotch-and-soda. To many of your fatuous admirers it seems an honour to be allowed to pay for your drinks at the "Pig and Whistle". Beware of such admirers.' He had a warning for younger players regarding their older team-mates, too: 'The beginner is only too apt to be led by the old stager. Tread warily when you first join the professional ranks.'

In 1909 Preston North End's Jimmy Wilson spoke candidly on these matters. 'We all know the bugbear of a footballer's career is alcohol,' he cautioned, 'Perhaps it is not generally known to how great an extent such a state of affairs does exist. One has only to make his way to one or two well-known hotels to see it for themselves.' Jimmy Costley, who played for Blackburn Olympic, was only too aware; his granddaughter later recalled that 'wherever he went people would buy him a drink and he would come home drunk'. Costley later signed 'the pledge' and became teetotal, although, in mitigation for his earlier actions, we might want to consider that Blackburn Olympic had a dietary schedule for its players before big games which involved consuming a glass of port at 6am. Still, that was not as detrimental as attending a wedding reception the night before one match was to Leicester Fosse, who suffered the indignity of a 12-0 loss to compound their collective hangover.

Looking upon such events, our old friend the anonymous columnist 'Football Secretary' in *Thomson's Weekly News* shared the same concerns as Jimmy Wilson about the influence of hangers-on. 'Footballers have a weakness for celebrating victory in their own way,' he wrote. 'It is often a case of "deliver me from my friends" for "friends" (so-called) spoil many a player; they're ever ready to treat him to a drink and then he ofttimes knows not when to stop.'

❧❧

While players – especially those from the north-west – had a relaxed attitude to drinking, many of the men who shaped football's earliest institutions (the Football Association and the Football League) stood in strong opposition to the taking of alcohol. William McGregor, a founder of the Football League in 1888, was a highly religious teetotaller. As secretary of Aston Villa, he would invite players he suspected of being fond of a tipple to meet with him in a coffee house every Monday morning where he would extol the virtues of sobriety to his weary audience. In his own words, McGregor stood for 'strict temperance in all things' and may have been attracted to the stewardship of the Birmingham club's affairs because of their roots in the Villa

Cross Wesleyan Chapel. He too was a Methodist, albeit with some Congregationalist instincts.

Born in Braco, Perthshire, and possessing a big white beard which gave him a distinctly Santa-At-The-Match vibe, McGregor was a man of relatively humble means, particularly when compared to benefactors of rival clubs during this era. Rather than a vast business empire, he owned a drapery shop nearby. The club, however, was cash-strapped when he arrived and could not afford to be choosy as to its owner. Nevertheless, both parties must have been delighted with the outcome when Villa went on to win the league five times between 1894 and 1900.

It was country rather than club which inadvertently got him into a tricky situation. While he was on Football Association business in Budapest, he had the misfortune of accidentally getting wasted! Given his deeply held beliefs, he had requested sparkling water when his Hungarian hosts had offered him champagne. Yet his request was misunderstood and, instead, he was offered something a little more medicinal. After spending most of the following day in bed, he informed one enquirer as to his well-being, 'I can assure you it was not sham pain!'

Charles Sutcliffe was another man of similar mind, a solicitor who played for Burnley and went on to influence the Football League as an administrator over the next four decades. Although teetotal, Sutcliffe saw himself as a man of the people in opposition to the snooty southern amateurs of Eton and Harrow. Notably, after an England international match he was asked by another administrator in the official FA motor-coach who a third figure, B.M.

Glanvill, represented, and he replied, 'The public schools.' Who then, asked his interlocutor, do we represent? 'The public houses,' Sutcliffe informed him.

Another strict Methodist who even refrained from reading a newspaper at home of a Sunday, he did have one vice: smoking. He did that a lot, puffing away on 60 'Senior Service' cigarettes a day. Like McGregor, he was active in the Liberal party as president of his local branch. Sutcliffe's playing career had ended around 1886, giving him more time to dedicate to his politics, his administrative roles within football and campaigning work on behalf of the temperance movement, particularly the Curzon Street Mission in his native Burnley.

Charles Clegg, some time chairman of both Sheffield Wednesday and Sheffield United, was another advocate of clean living. Known as the 'Napoleon of football', he eventually rose to the role of chairman of the Football Association. It was while at Wednesday that Clegg set a strictly enforced rule that his players could neither work nor live in a licensed premises. When one of his players, an F.H. Crenshaw, became a publican, the player was discharged from his footballing responsibilities. Another player was discovered drunk and disorderly in public, earning himself a one-month suspension with his wages docked. At Sheffield United, players living in the city were required to attend the club's billiards room on Wednesday, Thursday and Friday evenings in order to keep them out of mischief and would be disciplined if they failed to show up without good reason.

Given Clegg's background, all of this was unsurprising. He was president of Band of Hope, an organisation that had been founded in nearby Leeds in 1847 after the death of a young man through causes related to his drinking. Its aims were, ostensibly, to teach children about the evils of alcohol and the virtues of sobriety and soon it was holding meetings across the UK to spread this message. By 1891 two million members had signed its pledge of sobriety, illustrating the strength of temperance societies in the last two decades of the 19th century. Later, Clegg would become president of the British Temperance League.

John Lewis, a founder of Blackburn Rovers, was another football administrator who forged a similar path. He promoted the Sunday Football Movement – designed to keep working men out of the pubs on the Sabbath – which for many was their only full day away from their job. The son of a Methodist preacher, Lewis was an active campaigner against alcohol and himself devout in his faith. His sister Elizabeth Ann had set up the Lees Hall Teetotal Mission in Blackburn and he pursued these same objectives with a Puritanical zeal. One newspaper described him as 'straight as a die and absolutely fearless. His great ambition was to keep football sweet and clean.'

Lewis's own playing career had been ended by a skating accident (before which he was noted for his speed), but he went on to become a referee, officiating more than 1,000 games including three FA Cup finals. He fell out with a lot of people, and not just on the pitch. Regarded as being somewhat pompous and self-righteous, he saw football as an effective tool to mould both good men and, in turn, a great nation. The *Daily Dispatch* reported that he 'hardly missed an opportunity to speak out against drinking, smoking and gambling. This irritated many, but those who got to know him grew fond of him … He was, in short, a Puritan, living hundreds of years after his time.' Lewis himself remarked, 'I have ever worked hard – and played hard. It is an excellent combination. Add to it that I am a life abstainer and have never felt the slightest inclination for what is picturesquely called the "fragrant weed" and you have the recipe for my health and vigorous constitution.'

Not only was he the man in black, but he was a boy in blue too, being employed as a special constable. Yet despite his many jobs, Lewis never, ever missed church or, indeed, the opportunity to lecture on the evils of drink. On one FA jaunt around England, he covered 2,200 miles in 15 days but still managed to go to church on both Sundays, during which he was on the road. On another occasion, he was accused of being drunk while refereeing a match, a jibe which so infuriated Lewis that he threw off his jacket and squared up to his accuser. Neither did he confine his opinions solely to football, suggesting the English cricket team would have done better in Australia if they had refrained from imbibing while on tour.

❧❧

Lewis and his ilk were not the only founders and chairmen who liked to run a tight ship as far as boozing was concerned. Arnold Hills, founder of Thames Ironworks FC, was keen to use his wealth and influence to enforce abstemiousness and football was a sport he had some familiarity with, having gained a single England cap against Scotland in 1879. He saw the creation of this new club as 'a fresh link of interest and fellowship between all sorts and conditions of workers in our great industrial community' in which a company-approved temperance choir already existed. Together, these were institutions aimed at fostering an environment where wholesome leisure could flourish.

He was an influential figure in the sphere of late Victorian society which he inhabited. In 1888 Mahatma Gandhi had arrived in London to study law and became involved with the London Vegetarian Society. Eventually, he rose to sit on its executive committee, alongside its president, Mr Arnold Hills. Indeed, Gandhi wrote of his friend, 'The President of the Society was Mr Hills, proprietor of the Thames Iron Works. He was a puritan. It may be said that the existence of the Society depended practically on his financial assistance. Many members of the Committee were more or less his proteges.' When, in 1931, Gandhi returned to London for a short time, Hills was deceased but, residing in the East End, Gandhi is said to have supped on cream sodas in the Boleyn pub and taken in several West Ham fixtures.

It had been on 2 June 1895 that the *Thames Iron Works Gazette* published the following snippet that announced their intention to explore new sporting pursuits: 'Mr Taylor, who is working in the shipbuilding department, has undertaken to get up a football club for next winter and I learn that quoits and bowls will also be added to the attractions of the Hermit Road ground ...' Though much of the money to finance these activities came from Hills, workers were required to contribute a small subscription.

Francis Payne, company secretary of Ironworks, became the football club's chairman, as well as fulfilling his role as vice president of the company's Temperance League. The first incarnation of the team was entirely comprised of a squad of teetotal non-smokers, and even when they became West Ham just a few years later the side were still referred to by their opposition and in the press as 'the Teetotallers' for some time.

They were, it should be noted, not alone at this time in fielding a team of men who shunned a tipple. Bell's Temperance, a not insignificant presence in Lancastrian football, had come out of a working men's club in Accrington, which did not serve alcohol so they were consequently known as 'the Abstainers'. Similarly, when the like-minded Glasgow Northern FC visited England they sent a missive back home from Bootle which noted with some dismay that the pubs were open on a Sunday 'but the liquids we despised'.

As was the trend at the time, a committee of workers had taken over the day-to-day business of the Ironworks footballing operation once it had been established. Yet when the Ironworks team became a separate limited company – West Ham United FC, in 1900 – Hills bought around a quarter of the shares and offered to pay outstanding debts. This was on the basis that, as a teetotaller himself, he was 'very keen on playing a teetotal eleven next season, and the experiment is worth trying if only to vindicate the rights of football employers to call their own tune after paying the piper'. After Hills had made this proposition, the *Licensing World* trade publication had greeted his words with incredulity, calling it 'one of the most impudent attempts ever made to propagate the milk and water doctrine ... This is offering a premium on hypocrisy with a vengeance ... the Thames Ironworks F.C had far better remain in debt than accede to it.'

The policy, it transpired, was not enforced and Hills shed formal ties with the club a few seasons later, but West Ham continued with their approach of looking after the wages of players they suspected of having a drink problem. Practices like this were not entirely unusual; before the First World War some clubs would fulfil the role of employer but also a quasi-parental place in their players' lives. The 'Football Secretary' columnist wrote in 1901 that 'some players require as much looking after as little children, perhaps more so because children can be slapped when they're naughty and footballers can't.' The FA – with this as one among many considerations – introduced a maximum wage of £4 in the same year.

Despite the club's best efforts they could not, of course, regulate the entirety of the personal lives of even some of the most notable figures in their history. Syd King played for West Ham between 1899 and 1903 and was appointed secretary at the start of his final season as a player, which effectively installed him into a managerial role that he had already informally taken on. This was a man who was the opposite of the austere Hills, an archetypal East End bloke who liked a cigar and carried himself with a swagger. He remained in the hot seat for an astonishing 30 years, overseeing West Ham's election to the Football League from the Southern League in 1919.

In the season that followed his rise to the status of shareholder in the club, however, results were poor and the team returned to the Second Division. On 5 November 1932 they had already lost nine games in the new season and King was called before the board, where he appeared 'drunk and insubordinate'. It was well known that he was partial to a drink and, though they had been tolerant until this point, the next day he was removed from his post. He was suspended without pay for three months, told that he was not allowed into the Boleyn ground and granted an *ex gratia* payment of £3 a week.

A month after being sacked, Syd King was dead. Money was not a worry but his reputation had been shattered, whispers of illicit payments having contributed to his downfall. The coroner's inquest concluded that he had killed himself while of 'unsound mind', afflicted by delusions of persecution and paranoia. His demise was ultimately via an alcoholic drink laced with a corrosive liquid.

3.

DOWN AND OUT IN LA MANGA AND ST ETIENNE

'Footballers are no different to human beings'
– Graham Taylor

'THIS is fucking stupid,' a Geordie voice roared. 'I'm not having this. I don't do waiting.' Paul Gascoigne charged into a room where Ray Clemence, Glenn Roeder and John Gorman were sitting. He could tell from his friend Roeder's eyes that Glenn Hoddle was not going to take him to the tournament. That was when he exploded, bursting into the Royal Suite – Hoddle's room at the Hyatt Regency – where the manager was informing Phil Neville that he had not made the cut.

The music of Kenny G played quietly through a hi-fi in the background. 'What the fucking hell are you doing?' he yelled. 'You know what it means to me, you fucking bastard.'

Hoddle began to offer a justification but Gascoigne was having none of it. 'I don't want to hear any fucking explanations. I don't care what your reasons are. You know what you're fucking doing to me? You are a fucking bastard,' he shouted as he kicked a wardrobe door and overturned a small table, smashing a pottery vase and a lamp and cutting his own leg in the process. Hoddle tried again to reason with him: 'Gazza, your head isn't right.' The 31-year-old player told him, 'Just fucking shut up, you bastard.' Michael Owen – whose appointment with Hoddle was scheduled after Gascoigne's – later joked that 'walking into Glenn's room, I was so nervous about my slot but also wanting to look around to see what damage he'd done'.

In the weeks before the team travelled to their training camp in La Manga in the Murcian region of Spain, Gascoigne had been spotted staggering out of a kebab shop – apparently the worse for wear – alongside his celebrity mates Danny Baker and Chris Evans. A photographer had been poised nearby and the *Daily Mirror* ran it on their front page. Gascoigne was drunk again that afternoon in Spain, so the story goes, though in *Gazza,* he refuted that claim: 'I wasn't drunk. Not at all,' he wrote. 'I might have had a couple of beers earlier that morning on the golf course, but I certainly wasn't drunk. Perhaps a bit hungover from the night before, but that was all.'

❦

For anyone under the age of 40, the 1990s was an exciting time. Tony Blair's star was ascendant. Entering prime ministerial office in 1997 aged only 43, he was the youngest prime minister to be elected since 1812. As well as Evans,

Radio 1 presenters Zoe Ball and Sara Cox heralded a new era of lairiness that blew away the cobwebs of the stuffy, staid personalities who had passed for cultural titans in the early part of that decade when John Major had sat atop the governmental pyramid. Lad – and ladette – culture was seen as synonymous with 'Cool Britannia'. Blair even invited Oasis to Downing Street in an effort to ingratiate himself with these new icons and absorb some cool by osmosis. Football was part of this revolution too; it had been sanitised and glamorised from the doldrums it had found itself in after Thatcher's demonisation. Blair got in on the act here too, declaring himself (perhaps too enthusiastically) as a supporter of Newcastle United and participating in a spot of head tennis with Kevin Keegan. Gascoigne, in part through his association with Baker and Evans, was football's representative in this circus.

Alongside Jimmy 'Five Bellies' Gardiner, it was Baker and Evans who were the non-footballers most closely associated with Gascoigne's drinking escapades during the 1990s. Evans hosted *TFI Friday*'s initial run of 179 episodes from February 1996 until December 2000 on Channel 4, a programme deeply symbolic of the times in which it aired: brash, bawdy and boozy. Though Americans were rapidly moderating their drinking habits during the late 90s, Brits were careening merrily in the opposite direction. Depending on your point of view, the Baker-Evans duo could be seen as enablers and encouragers of Gascoigne's behaviour. Baker in particular, ten years the footballer's senior, should have known better. Gascoigne, of course, was not a child and was capable of making his own mistakes, as he quite obviously demonstrated. Yet a feeling lingered that they should have seen the state their friend was slipping into and, perhaps, put the brakes on some of their wilder antics.

❧

Gascoigne's nightmare in La Manga had begun the night before his explosion in Hoddle's hotel room. The players would be informed if they had earned a place in the squad on Sunday, but on the Saturday evening Hoddle gave the players an opportunity to relax and have a few drinks. For two of the party, drinking was not on the list of approved activities. In Paul Merson's own words, he and Tony Adams spent the evening 'eating sarnies and having the odd cuppa' around the resort. For the St Albans man, a few months after his 30th birthday, it was the first tournament he had been involved in where getting drunk would not feature in proceedings. Despite being a reformed character by then, he had been omitted from Venables's Euro 96 side after blotting his copybook early on in El Tel's reign.

In his account of the tournament, Merson wondered about the wisdom of Hoddle's laissez-faire approach to that evening's refreshment situation. 'I didn't see the need for [the night of permitted drinking],' he wrote. 'For Gazza, it was like a red rag to a bull.' When he and Adams had looked in around 9pm, Gascoigne was playing the piano, beckoning them to come and have a drink with him. Later, he would perform a karaoke rendition of Elvis Presley's 'Wooden Heart' before teasing, 'Come on Tone, give us a song, you boring bastard.' The party in the 'Blue Oyster

Bar' would eventually break up at one o'clock on Sunday morning.

Merson and Adams had become roommates when England were on the road, best able to understand one another's whims as men who were both relatively new to sobriety. At La Manga, they had a room each but shared a kitchen and lounge. During the tournament itself they watched *U.S. Marshals*, a sequel to *The Fugitive*, and would read an item of Alcoholics Anonymous literature, *Day By Day*, together each morning.

On that Sunday – decision day for Hoddle – Merson had spent some time playing bowls with Dion Dublin. Hoddle had arranged a short slot for each player to come and see him in his room, beginning with David Seaman at 4.15pm. Gascoigne was due in at 5.15pm, while Merson's and Adams's appointments were scheduled after 6pm. Around four o'clock that afternoon, he and Adams were having tea and scones when a seemingly drunk Gascoigne had reappeared. The midfielder, by now a Middlesbrough player, had been on the golf course with Paul Ince, David Seaman, Ian Walker and Phil Neville. He was said to have purchased a few cans along the way, despite strict instructions to restrict his intake to zero.

When he returned to the complex, some players were amused but Merson and Adams were not among them. They stripped Gascoigne's clothes off and threw him into the swimming pool in an attempt to sober him up before his one-to-one with Hoddle. As they forced some coffee down his throat, Gascoigne was downbeat. 'This is shit,' he lamented. 'I've gone, I can't do it anymore.' He struck a despairing, despondent note: 'I can't believe it's come to this. I don't know if I can do it anymore. I'm not going to go, am I Tone?' Merson tried to lighten the mood, joking with Gascoigne that if he was not selected by Hoddle he would probably smash his room up. It was an interjection which Gascoigne later blamed for planting the idea in his head.

When FA press officer Steve Double came down a while later to tell some of the players that he had heard the Geordie would not be going to France, Gascoigne was upstairs in Hoddle's room. By the time Merson had arrived on the scene and David Seaman was already there, offering comforting words and reassuring Gascoigne that he still had what it took. As Merson put it, it was 'stuff he didn't need to hear'. Seaman had been a strong influence on Gascoigne during their fishing sessions together and he had warned him two years earlier – before Euro 96 – that his behaviour was letting his team-mates down. In Merson's view, 'tough-love reality' was required again in order to bring Gascoigne to a place where he could 'wise up and do something before it was all too late'.

In the short term, Merson found Gary Lewin to come and tend to Gascoigne's bloody leg, a wound incurred during the commotion of that late afternoon. Seaman and Ince had arrived just in time, with Gascoigne intent on smashing the windows of Hoddle's room, only becalmed by the team doctor dispensing some Valium. The next day, he was on the first plane out of Murcia along with Phil Neville, Ian Walker, Dion Dublin, Andy Hinchcliffe and Nicky Butt. Back in Blighty, he went to stay with his wife Sheryl, from whom he would shortly be divorced. He chose not to watch a single minute of the World Cup.

Paul Merson's inclusion was confirmed, yet he worried that he was only going because Gascoigne had made himself unpickable. 'You were both on that plane,' Hoddle assured him. After that, his feelings turned to guilt that he was going and his friend was not. Michael Owen believed Hoddle would have been asking for trouble taking Gascoigne only to put him on the bench: 'Glenn was going with Scholesy as his playmaker, and he probably thought if Gazza is not in the starting 11, what was he going to be like?'

Merson remained critical of Hoddle's methods. He believed that telling the players on an individual basis while they were still at the training camp was bad for the psychology of some of the team, particularly Gascoigne. He described the experience as 'one that I don't think any potential England squad member should be put through' so close to the start of a tournament. Adams concurred, writing in his second autobiography that 'Gazza was an ill man and Glenn did not understand properly the illness of addiction even if he tried to deal with it in the best way he knew how.' Hoddle was just 40 himself in 1998, a relatively inexperienced manager, and seemed to lack the interpersonal nous to deal with his most complicated of players.

When the team convened at Burnham Beeches to prepare for the tournament, Merson's first action was to be voluntarily drug-tested to put himself above reproach. Teddy Sheringham had decided to head straight back to the Iberian peninsula for the week the players had been given off before the pre-tournament preparations began in earnest. He was pictured in a nightclub on the Algarve with his arm around a blonde woman and a cigarette in his mouth while technically still on England duty. Merson could only laugh. 'Four years ago it would have been me,' he said. Instead, aged 30, he had never felt fitter. Sheringham had been nicknamed 'Charlie' by Merson and Adams after this incident, in part because he had had his hair cut short and looked like his own ten-year-old son, and also because of his perceived 'boyish' behaviour in jetting off to Portugal.

The tournament – when it eventually arrived – was notable from an English perspective for David Beckham's red card, brandished after a petulant flick of the leg towards Diego Simeone in a game that Hoddle's men lost on penalties. On their way to the exit, they had contended with Tunisia in their opening group game, recording a 2-0 victory via goals from Alan Shearer and Paul Scholes. Afterwards, Gareth Southgate declared, 'We celebrated victory with quite a few drinks … of coke and orange that is!' Next up were Romania, against whom England lost despite Michael Owen's valiant equaliser in the 83rd minute. This meant that the final group fixture in which Colombia were their opponents would be crucial to their progress. Goals from Darren Anderton and Beckham ensured this was the case, setting up that quarter-final tie against Argentina.

After the tournament, Paul Gascoigne sold his version of events at La Manga to *The Sun*, a move that Merson criticised. He believed that his colleague 'wallow[ed] in the details', a trait seen as familiar among alcoholics. Merson was in no doubt that he and his friend were suffering from the same illness, particularly after they had spent time as housemates during the last three months of the previous season at Middlesbrough. As the 1998/99 season dawned, Gascoigne was unfit and still blaming Merson for planting the idea of smashing up Hoddle's room into his head. Merson had a gut feeling that something bad was looming on his own horizon, fearing a return to the old patterns of behaviour which had seen him lose large sums of money through gambling, drinking and cocaine use. '[It was] difficult being around Gazza at that time,' Merson wrote. 'He had come to live with me after his move from Rangers. He liked a drink in the house …'

For a man with the challenges he faced, it was a regrettable situation for Merson, during which he admitted 'los[ing] sight of [his] own problems'. Where Tony Adams was a healthy, positive influence, Gascoigne was the opposite. Merson saw the latter as prone to pointing the finger at other people and blaming members of the press for his problems rather than confronting his demons. He explained that 'they are, though, just excuses to keep drinking'. The winger believed that 'when the excuses stop, that's when recovery will start', but did not think that would happen until the mercurial Gascoigne had retired from football. Adams was philosophical – 'his path was not my path' – but not angry, feeling only sadness at his friend's predicament.

As the 1998/99 Premier League season progressed, things only got worse for Gascoigne. On 10 October he was found sobbing on a platform at Stevenage railway station after returning from a bender with friends in Dublin. He was persuaded to go into the Priory, initially agreeing to stay for one night. Merson advised Middlesbrough boss Bryan Robson 'you've got to be firm with him' and that the club had to show some tough love to their star. It was a sobering reminder for Merson of just where his own addiction could take him and 'how devastating this illness can be'. His consistent desire throughout the entire episode was that the kid gloves needed to be cast aside. When the FA's David Davies rang Merson to see if he would do a press conference about Gascoigne's predicament, he agreed only on the condition he could speak frankly.

Getting Gascoigne into treatment was one thing but getting him to stay was quite another. Again, Merson was a key influence, albeit with a little help from Eric Clapton. The day after Gascoigne had been admitted to the Priory, Merson was visiting his friend and was asked by a member of staff if he minded whether the musician joined them in Gascoigne's room. When Clapton asked the patient if he drank alone, he responded that he 'like[d] half a bottle of wine in front of the telly', deploying, as Merson described, 'the alcoholic's understatement'. After the rocker had departed, Merson asked Gascoigne what he would do if Bryan Robson was to tell him he would have to stay there beyond that day. His reply? 'I'd leave the club.'

Gascoigne was, of course, duly informed that he needed to stay under the care of the experts at the Priory for a week and – with some encouragement from Merson – agreed that he would. It was a constant battle: after another week, he agreed to stay for a further seven days. It was all familiar territory for Merson, who wrote that he 'recognised that horrible space [Gascoigne] was in'. At one point, Gascoigne rang Merson and asked if *he* was alright. 'Yeah, I've had a Red Bull and a wine gum,' Merson joked with him.

A less cheerful phone call followed two days later. Gascoigne wanted out again and this time he went through with it, albeit with the caveat that he would go back as an outpatient twice a week. He believed that training and playing football would help him navigate his route to a more stable situation. Merson was adamant with Middlesbrough's manager, Bryan Robson, that Gascoigne should not be permitted to blame the press for his troubles, as he had done on previous occasions. They were not the ones picking up a drink, the footballer was. A press conference followed, at which Gascoigne announced he was never going to drink again. Merson wished he had chosen another form of words. 'What he should have said was, "I'm just not going to have a drink today."'

4.

A CUP OF PLENTY

HAVING plateaued for a few years, beer sales fell by 20 per cent between 1874 and 1886. Breweries needed to create new patterns of drinking rather than replicate the older ones, which were withering away as employment patterns and living standards improved.

The prospect of large groups of men gathering at a fixed, central location was a positive in terms of their potential profitability. Encouraging fans to continue drinking on their premises – rather than one tied to a rival brewery – was something these companies took seriously. They set up savings clubs for fans which could be drawn upon in order to attend cup finals and big away fixtures. Pubs would also provide updates on the score and other information from the match when the team was playing away: the Scarborough Hotel in Leeds boasted of its ability to provide bulletins every ten minutes for high-profile fixtures. As well as this, pubs began selling the rapidly delivered 'football special' newspapers that would arrive a few hours after that afternoon's games had concluded. In 1908 the Mitchell and Butler brewery – also a major source of loans to West Bromwich Albion – held several board meetings discussing precisely which paper to supply in their tied outlets.

Breweries were also keen to entice former players (usually those who had been local stars) to take up a tenancy in one of their premises. This was a job reserved for the elite performers of the day, who could expect to continue in this line of work for a decade after they had hung up their boots. It was a practice that only went into decline – before completely disappearing – after World War Two, just as amateur clubs became wise to the possibility of using the social clubs attached to their stands for commercial purposes.

Acting strategically, breweries located their tied pubs around pockets of support in their city and, it scarcely needs to be said, close to the ground. Whitbread's, for example, were quick to invest £35,000 in the White Hart Inn, situated next to Tottenham's ground, on land which was itself leased from the brewery. The formation of the Football League in 1888 had led to a sharp rise in crowds at football matches as the game took on a more competitive edge. Clubs needed to build stands to accommodate these new supporters, a reality which required substantial and rapid investment.

Watford, later owned by reformed drunk Elton John, had financial support from the Benskins brewery, who provided them with capital to acquire their Cassio Road ground and later their present-day base at Vicarage Road. Benskins also loaned the club £12,000 in order to bring it up to a presentable state in exchange for ten per cent of the gate receipts. When the football club encountered financial difficulties in 1926, the brewery once again stepped in to pay off its debts. The footballing operation even became known as 'The Brewers' for a period of their history.

These companies were often happy to oblige in funding football clubs because, in addition to benefitting trade in their premises around the ground, it allowed them to have their name painted across the top of the stands their cash had helped construct. After the First World War, the breweries – and the drinks industry as a whole – had found themselves in a parlous state. Hard-hitting measures were brought in by government because of the deleterious effect it was seen to have on the populace. Breweries responded by redoubling their efforts to exploit the opportunities that organised sport offered to their bottom line.

One such example of this practice is found in the Simond's brewery, who provided many loans to Reading FC in the 1920s, even as the odds of repayment by the club appeared to be diminishing. Their association with the club and the presence it gave in the area was a form of repayment in itself: their return on investment coming partly through footfall in their pubs. The same company became a shareholder in Wembley Stadium in 1927, buying 500 'one-shilling' shares. Soon after this cash injection they won the contract to provide refreshments at the new venue and the following decade would also become a lender to Tottenham Hotspur.

Another brewery, Brickwood's, shut down four of its pubs in Portsmouth in exchange for being able to open The Pompey near Fratton Park. At Brentford's Griffin Park, the ground's owners decided to keep it simple and buy the pubs situated on its four corners in order to pocket the revenues themselves. In the Midlands, Wolves (now unchained from their religious beginnings) leased Molineux from Northampton Brewers. Attempting to raise revenues, other clubs – notably Cardiff – had trouble fully utilising their home due to the landowner's objection to the possibility of drinking alcohol and gambling activities taking place there.

✿

Arsenal, one of the only professional sides in the south-east at this time, would soon face a similar challenge to their friends in Wales. In what was then a peripheral area of London, Arsenal's Manor ground in Woolwich was hard to access. The team itself had been relegated in the 1911/12 season with what was then the all-time worst points record for a top-flight team. In seeking to remedy this sporting malaise, the prospect of a move to north London meant they could tap into the potential of several hundred thousand people living across Finsbury, Hackney, Islington and Holborn. Happily for the club, there were six acres of land belonging to St John's College of Divinity that were potentially up for grabs, though some observers thought the Church of England would be loath to countenance its sale to a football club. Yet when Arsenal chairman Henry Norris – Conservative mayor of Fulham, Freemason and philanthropist – offered them £20,000 in 1913, they felt it was an offer they would be foolish to refuse. It was a decision perhaps aided by the fact that Norris was able to call the Archbishop of Canterbury a personal friend.

Originally, the plan had been to merge the Woolwich club with Fulham FC (a club Norris had also backed financially) and play at Craven Cottage. It was when this was met with opposition the relocation to Islington was actioned. Despite this, Norris – tall, thin and possessing a walrus-like moustache – remained a director at Fulham even while taking up the position of chairman at Arsenal. Having shed the Woolwich prefix upon this move, the club faced a similar dilemma: the church still owned the leasehold at their new location and the powers-that-be forbade matches on this land on Christmas Day and Good Friday. Even worse, they told the club that the sale of 'intoxicating liquor' within its confines was also out of the question. The club went along with this for a year before the lure of income from sales of alcohol to thirsty men became too strong and, in 1925, they acquired outright ownership of the site for £64,000.

⁂

Though we know the church played a part in the origins of many clubs across the country, in late-19th century south Lancashire allegiances between breweries and football clubs were also common. Some of these arrangements would go beyond piecemeal financial support in the form of loans and the footballing operation would, effectively, become a sister company of the brewing concern. One club, however, bucked this trend by turning away from their wealthy backer John Houlding because of his links to the licensed trade. It was Everton who, partly owing to their Methodist origins – having been formed from St Domingo's in 1878 – decided to cut ties with their benefactor.

After Houlding had raised the rent at Anfield and refused to sell it to the club, the *Liverpool Mercury* announced on 16 March 1892 that he had been removed from his position as president of the club during an emergency general meeting. Everton had won the league title in 1891 but had made a feeble effort defending it the following season. Some figures within the corridors of power thought that this was because the players got changed in the Sandon Hotel – a pub on Oakfield Road which you can still visit today – across the street from Anfield. Both premises were owned by Houlding and it was suggested that perhaps they were sampling its wares too liberally before taking the field.

Chief among Houlding's critics was George Mahon, a Liberal where Houlding was a Conservative. Drinking was a widespread phenomenon on the Liverpudlian streets, not least because – as was the case elsewhere at this time – beer was considered safer to drink than water. In 1853 the Liberal party and a number of churches had created the United Kingdom Alliance, a temperance movement with the goal of the prohibition of alcohol across the nation. Around Merseyside, many Conservative politicians had strong links to the drinks trade so, naturally, the finger of blame was pointed at them by their Liberal counterparts, who were slowly eating into their vote share. When the party were actually elected with prohibition featuring as a central plank in their platform, William Gladstone (himself born in Liverpool) found himself in a difficult position. He couldn't *actually* ban alcohol so instead he reduced the duty on French wine in the hope that the British and Irish populace would adopt a more continental approach to their libations.

His fellow Liberal Liverpudlian Mahon was teetotal, in stark contrast to Houlding who even had a Sparkling Ale product line carrying his name. By the age of 20, the latter man had been appointed chief brewer at the first firm he worked at and 17 years later he had saved enough money to buy his own brewery. Crucially, when he had acquired Anfield for the club for £6,000 (£350,000 in 2019 money), there had been no formal contract between himself and Everton, merely an agreement to repay the loan at four per cent when the club was in a sound position to do so. He continued to lend Everton further sums and became a Tory councillor.

The ringleader of Houlding's tormentors during the very public battle, Mahon blamed him for the club's slump after their league-winning season. Houlding had become aware of moves to oust him and had unsuccessfully attempted to set up another club bearing the Everton name. As a result of his personal control over the ground, a number of the club's directors wanted to move away from Anfield. He wanted to be rid of their influence in any case, so setting up a new legal entity seemed an efficient way of achieving this. When accusations had been put to him at the EGM, he had replied, 'I am here to reply, and a criminal never takes the chair, he steps into the dock.' Three days later, Liverpool Football Club and Athletic Grounds Limited was born, backed by an injection of cash from both the Threlfall and Bent brewery companies and later benefitting from the largesse of Tarbuck's brewery.

The new tenants at Anfield would have to wait another three months to be recognised by the FA. When their application to join the Football League was rejected without much consideration, they joined the Lancashire League instead. This reflected the reality that Everton, and even the (to our modern eye) lesser-known Bootle FC, were simply bigger, better supported clubs at this time.

Though in its earliest days there was acrimony between them – particularly when Liverpool triumphed in the first derby, in the Liverpool Senior Cup Final – the Merseyside rivalry would be described as an unusually friendly one for many decades to follow. In the 1930s there was some evidence of conviviality between their playing staff, during which Elisha Scott and Dixie Dean used to meet in a city-centre pub after most matches. It was a pint of bitter for Dixie while Scott opted for a Guinness. Before one Stanley Park encounter, it is said that Scott received a letter from Dean with two aspirins and a letter reading, 'You better get these down you. You'll need a good night's sleep, because I'll be scoring against you tomorrow.'

※

Though the business of alcohol was a key driver of early English football's development, it was not on this island but in Germany where alcohol brands would become a familiar sight on players' shirts, and so we will take a brief foray to continental Europe. Here we find Gunter Mast, the man responsible. Why not, he had wondered, replace the lion on the shirts worn by cash-strapped Eintracht Braunschweig's players with Jägermeister's stag? The DFB took some time to be convinced but by 1973 were eventually – begrudgingly – won over, despite protestations from its general secretary, Hans Passlack, that 'he makes our Bundesliga a pub'. It was a home fixture against Schalke 04 that saw the Frankfurt team enter the field in front of their 15,000 fans with the stag's antlers on their chests, where it would remain for the next 14 seasons.

Braunschweig's coach viewed the change – perhaps unsurprisingly – in a rather more positive light than the DFB official. 'This puts us on a par with clubs like Opel Rüsselsheim, Bayer Leverkusen, Mayer Landau, Bayer Uerdingen and Röchling Völklingen,' he said. Back then, it was worth what seems a frankly trifling amount to our modern eyes: just 100,000 Deutschmarks (worth around £45,000 in 2019). In 2016 it's thought that Fiat offered the same club around six million euros a year to have their badge emblazoned across their shirts. Despite the small sums involved, Mast was a pioneer. He recognised that the newly professionalised German league was ripe for exploitation and the five million marks that his company would go on to invest in the sport over the next decade or so represented 18 per cent of their total ad budget. Part of this value was derived from just how controversial this move was, a fact Mast was only too aware of. 'I prefer negative headlines,' he proclaimed, 'rather than positive coverage, the attention is higher.' The executive was instrumental in bringing Paul Breitner back to the Bundesliga for what was a record 1.6 million marks (in today's money, around £725,000). He had even tried to change the name of the club to Jägermeister

Braunschweig, though this faced insurmountable opposition in the German court system.

His revelatory moment had come when Mast had thrown a party at his house. At a certain point in proceedings, many of the guests had disappeared. He located them in front of a television set, his invitees glued to an international football match. Not long later he was in conversation with Ernst Fricke, then president of Eintracht, who were close to financial implosion. This, Mast thought, was an ideal opportunity.

Shirt sponsorship had been banned by the DFB six years previously when the Wormatia Worms had tried it, so they were forced to be creative. In the end, the logo itself was transformed from a lion into a stag. The authorities were powerless to stop this but decreed that club badges could measure no more than 14 centimetres. Braunschweig's sortie into 'sponsorship' heralded a new commercialised era of German football; Hamburger SV soon followed suit with a tie-in with Campari, and it would be just four years before shirt sponsorship reached English shores courtesy of Jimmy Hill's Coventry and the (now defunct) car manufacturer Talbot.

Amusingly, on the occasion of his 80th birthday, Mast would confess that he was not a much of a football fan, recognising it only for its marketability: 'I know when the ball goes into the goal, but I couldn't explain the offside rule to you.' Mast's crafty arrangement could not be made now. Soeren Oliver Voigt, Eintracht's president until 2018, has said, 'That would be a problem today. Despite the history, the product would simply no longer fit in with us.' The league has tightened its rules too and, in any case, Jägermeister themselves say on their own website that 'from the company's perspective, alcohol and sports do not mix'. Products with an ABV higher than 15 per cent can no longer grace the shirts of footballers in Germany and all tobacco products have been similarly consigned to the past.

❦

Though it would have been to the dismay of Hills, Clegg, Mahon and their acolytes nearly a century earlier, it was the Watney Cup that eventually brought alcohol sponsorship to the English game. This was in the early 1970s, in a competition that had the added distinction of being the first to use a penalty shootout to decide matches which would otherwise have had to have been replayed after ending in a draw. The Watney brewery paid £82,000 for the privilege of having its name – formally Watney Mann – attached to the invitational knockout cup, a short-lived Football League wheeze lasting four seasons between 1970 and 1973. It had taken two participants from each division, with qualification determined by plucking the two highest-scoring teams who had not otherwise been promoted or gained entry to European competition.

That this link between football and alcohol was not seen as controversial was in part because it was a peripheral competition. When the League Cup required a new benefactor in 1982, it was not to booze which it turned but milk, seen as suitably innocuous to be associated with when the Milk Marketing Board became the competition sponsor for the next four seasons. There were still some products which – even with a commercial imperative – would have been impolitic to be tied too closely with.

It was not until the 1990s that breweries and their brands became prevalent as sponsors of major trophies. In 1993 Bass entered the fray by securing the naming rights to the top flight, which became known as the FA Carling Premiership. Foster's had been proposed as a sponsor for the FA Cup, though this was shelved after an outcry provoked not so much by the tie-in with an alcohol company but by the notion of a commercial partnership at all. By 1998 Bass was spending more than £1 million a month on the Premiership alone, while also – via its Worthington arm – sponsoring the League Cup. Carlsberg had got involved too: first as shirt sponsor to Liverpool FC and later as the official beer of the FA Cup, the Cup Winners' Cup, the UEFA Cup and the England team during the 1998 World Cup.

It was certainly lucrative in terms of return on investment. During their sponsorship of England's top division, sales of Carling rose by 31 per cent – including a 76 per cent spike during Euro 96. In 1999 they became the first brewery to sell a billion pints in a single year. Some would credit them with helping to 'rebuild' English football after the doldrums of the 1980s. Similarly, Carlsberg could boast of selling three million pints in pubs during France 98, alongside a staggering 45 million cans during the same period. No wonder a representative from the Bass marketing department had declared, 'When football succeeds, so does the brand.'

5.

MYTHMAKING AND MERLOT

WHEN Paul Gascoigne accepted his award for Sports Book of the Year at the British Book Awards in April 2005, his words might have given hope that he had turned a corner. Among his remarks came the declaration, 'This is the third thing I've won in two years. I won against alcohol and drugs. The third is the book award. This one is for life – I just hope I can make sure the other two are as well.'

Recovering alcoholics of a certain strain might have bristled at his use of the word 'won', however rhetorical it was. Within 12-step fellowships like Alcoholics Anonymous, there is a belief that one does not 'win' the battle with alcohol until one's last breath, and that – on some level – it is always there 'doing press-ups' as it is often described among recovering members. Even so, the caveat that he hoped it would be for life boded well. He had admitted that he was an alcoholic, and that there was something there that needed to be dealt with. This is AA's step one: 'We admitted we were powerless over alcohol – that our lives had become unmanageable.' It does not of itself denote a course of action, but concedes that there may be a need for it.

Gascoigne had been sober for three months when the first edition of his autobiography was released. He was getting to three AA meetings a week following a 43-day spell in treatment at Sierra Tuscon. The facility in Arizona was famously loath to accommodate Gascoigne and Merson at the same time, waiting for the former to depart before admitting the latter. In *Gazza* he reflected that he had 'got an illness' but later wondered if it would 'turn [him] into a boring person', asking the reader, 'What if the penalty, the by-product, is to become a sensible, dreary, boring twat?' Many would argue that, even if true, this would be a price worth paying. There's a strain of thought that says that great alcoholic or otherwise addicted artists, musicians, thinkers and – yes – footballers would lose some of their essence, their flair, were they to go sober. That's one argument, of course, but another that seems more persuasive is that a fit and fighting Gascoigne would have been a better player who could perform with all the same verve and flair but, crucially, a more cooperative body.

The feting around boozers like Gascoigne and George Best as 'legends' for their antics – such as the singing of songs by Northern Ireland fans, to the tune of 'Spirit in the Sky' about 'going on the piss with Georgie Best' – and the media idolisation of these figures even when the tragic results are plain to see, seem a particularly crass form of adulation. Yet the notion – the *myth* – of this romantic ideal of the footballing alcoholic has a deep hold in sections of society. As Henry Winter put it in his exploration of the England national team *50 Years of Hurt*, 'We all laugh obediently, sadly keeping Gascoigne pigeonholed as Gazza.'

Players like Gascoigne become cartoonish figures to us. We think they have it made and often we wish we could live their lives. The realities of their situations, the paranoia, the delusions, are mostly hidden from view. Like Winter, I have very consciously refrained from referring to Gascoigne as 'Gazza' throughout this book. To do so is to play into the stereotype, to indulge the hangers-on around him and the cheerleaders for his lifestyle and, by extension, the man himself. It's almost as if we expect him to play up to it, demanding a charade from him: his fishing rod, some KFC and a six pack. By doing so, we play into these games, feeding our own desire for these clownish figures to be packaged into our media diet. Poignantly, Gascoigne wrote in his own autobiography in 2005 that he thought the 'Gazza stage in [his] life could be over.' If only it had been.

The media, of course, is often used by Gascoigne as a reason why he started drinking again, could not stop, or otherwise carried on boozing as normal. In *My Story,* he writes of the press, 'for ten years they had been looking out for me, ignoring other players out on the town'. That other players are often featured across the front and back pages of the newspapers seems not to matter. Nor does the fact that, in most cases, their drinking escapades were neither as sustained or severe as Gascoigne's. There is undoubtedly soul-searching that needs to take place around the media's dealings with Gascoigne, but he cannot pin his alcoholism on to them. As Merson observed of his friend's notoriety, he 'used it as a reason for failing to sustain his own recovery from alcoholism'.

There is a consistent thread of self-pity that runs through Gascoigne's musings on his circumstances. In one passage he rails at the media, 'I just wanted a decent life and to enjoy football. I didn't become a professional footballer so I could get to be hounded to bits for the rest of my life, and I've not played for 12 years. What have I done to deserve this? I ended up an alcoholic. Just leave us alone.' This fits into a wider theme of excusing his own behaviour. By the time the paperback version of his autobiography was released he was nearly two years sober. However, he had not gone to an AA meeting for the previous two months because of being in and out of hospital: 'I haven't been able to, have I?' Elsewhere in this edition of the book, he writes about his ex-wife, Sheryl, an airing of laundry that serves only as an attempt to absolve himself of responsibility and minimise his own actions.

Tony Adams had tried to counsel Gascoigne about his drinking on the flight back from a friendly in Morocco in 1998 but wrote, 'There's nothing you can do if somebody doesn't want it.' Adams suspected that after he had climbed on the wagon a couple of years previously, Gascoigne had 'perhaps … started to look at me as if I was on a different planet. He couldn't make out what I was about.' In a wider footballing context, Adams thought, 'Managers have turned a blind eye to some of his antics down the years as long as he performed on the pitch, but I'm not sure they have all done him a favour.'

There were managers who Gascoigne seemed to connect with too. Among those with whom he had an understanding were Walter Smith, Bobby Robson and Terry Venables. Before one England match, Gascoigne had been fretting about his broken bath at home and, knowing that it was playing on his player's mind, Venables phoned a plumber for him in order that he could play the match with this apparently heavy weight off his mind. Instinctively, he knew how to handle his star.

It's clear that Venables gave Gascoigne a little more leeway than anyone else in the squad. Where Merson was iced, Gascoigne was included. Venables knew how to get the best out of him – on and off the pitch – because they liked and respected one another. He could see that Gascoigne lifted the mood of most of his team-mates. For Gareth Southgate, Gascoigne was a player that 'everyone who played with him loved'. That future England manager also described his Euro 96 compatriot as 'a very generous person, a warm person. He would do anything for anybody. Sadly, that was abused by some people.' Alan Shearer's description of him as 'one of the most misunderstood people I have ever known' struck a similar tone.

Bobby Robson got him too. The image of Gascoigne at Italia 90 is iconic, but it was also among his happiest times in football. He loved being at that World Cup, 'It was everything I wished for, how I wanted life to be,' he wrote. Gascoigne had friends and team-mates around 24 hours a day 'to play with', able to forget any 'boring' or 'domestic' obligations for the duration of the tournament. This was even better than playing for Spurs, since there he would have nothing to do after training. As such, his tears after his sending off in the semi-final against West Germany must be seen in this context: not just his grief at missing a potential final, but because it came with the realisation that he would soon have to go home. This was the same tournament during which Gascoigne was caught by Robson playing five sets of late-night tennis with a fellow hotel guest the evening before a match. Chris Waddle was Gascoigne's roommate in Italy in 1990 and reflected wryly, 'That's Gazza! He had energy, he was hyperactive. He never slept a lot. Every light had to be on. Telly had to be on.'

The drinking was not seen as serious at this stage. There was still an ability to laugh along in good conscience at Gascoigne's japes, most notably his donning of the fake breasts and hairy chest. When he was transferred to Italy to play for Lazio a few years later, the culture was different. He writes that he 'hardly got drunk at all' in the land of Calcio. It was, he thinks, when he went to Rangers that his drinking became serious. At that time, he had not fully grasped that alcohol was a depressant but 'it was all I wanted to do. Anything to stop my head going round and round.'

During the spell in the Priory that followed in the months after moving to Middlesbrough, he shouted at Sheryl 'I'm not a fucking alcoholic!' Instead of throwing himself into treatment, he stayed for three weeks rather than a month but attended only about as many AA meetings during that time. As he acknowledged in *Gazza*, 'I wouldn't admit I was an alcoholic; instead I vowed to stay off the drink, never again to touch another drop.' Writing several years later, he had decided to dedicate himself to getting sober. He explained, 'I know that when I put my mind to something, I can do it. It's just another form of excess, after all.' The excess, in this case, was attendance at meetings and committing to a new lifestyle. It was a marked difference from that first spell in the Priory, during which he had only missed two Middlesbrough games – far fewer than Merson missed during his ban or Adams during his injury layoff that coincided with his sobering up – a fact that he seemed strangely proud of: 'I suppose I looked upon football as the best cure, the one aspect of my life that has always kept me focussed, cleared my head of all my worries and phobias, allowed me to escape from my worst self.'

❄❄❄

'I'm not a fucking alcoholic!' There are many terms that get thrown around when it comes to drink, drinking and drinkers: lout, glutton, yob, pisshead, waster, lightweight, *alcoholic*. Yes, that's the one that tends to sting the most, particularly when one does not – or does not *want to* – believe that it is so. The word itself, which in its original meaning used to refer to an inebriated person, came into common usage in the late 19th century and was widely understood to refer to 'habitual drunkenness' by 1910.

Before that, there had been other words that had carried similar baggage. The Scottish physician Alexander Peddie, writing in the 1850s, used the term 'dipsomania' – coined by the German-Russian doctor C. von Brühl-Cramer in 1819 and literally meaning 'manic thirst' – to describe a mental phenomenon he saw as 'symptomatic of some abnormal cerebral condition which gives it the form of insanity', brought on not 'by intoxicating drinks, as it [was] that which created the desire for them'. Peddie's solution was simple: the dipsomaniac should be 'suitably restrained since he can no longer control himself'.

While in its earliest form dipsomania was used to allude to drinking characterised by bouts, the term alcoholism – used to describe longer-term drinking – was conceived by Magnus Huss in 1849. Norman Kerr, a doctor who was active in the British Temperance Society, preferred the term 'inebriety', seeing it as a 'diseased state of the brain and nervous centres, characterised by an irresistible impulse to indulge in intoxicating liquors or other narcotics, for the release which these afford, at any peril'. Speaking at the society's inaugural meeting in 1884, he emphasised his strongly held belief that what he was talking about was a medical rather than moral failing. 'I have not attempted to dogmatize on disputed points as to whether inebriety is a sin, a vice, a crime, or a disease,' he wrote. 'In my humble judgement, it is sometimes all four, but oftener a disease than anything else, and even when anything else, generally a disease as well.'

Hugh Wingfield, another physician, claimed 'the normal man is not, and cannot be subject to the temptation faced by alcoholics'. There were many furrowed brows in the late 19th century as people pontificated as to whether, if this was a disease, the diseased person had some responsibility for finding themselves in this position. Some judges saw it as a 'madness for which the madman is to blame'. Another member of the legal profession, wrestling with this quandary, opined, 'If a vice, it might be prosper to punish it. If a disease, it might be possible to cure it.'

When Gascoigne returned to the side after his attempt to 'check', if not 'cure' his condition, he was half a stone lighter and given a warm reception by the Middlesbrough faithful. The rehab process had clearly benefitted him and he was awarded Man of the Match by the television commentators at the conclusion of the game. Yet as the season drew to a close, he had started drinking again – privately, at home – choosing vodka because, like so many, he believed it would be harder to detect on his breath. When Sheryl gave an interview to *The Sun*, this was more fuel to his fire: 'No wonder I was tempted to have a drink or three, with all that going on.' Elton John offered him a house to stay in to get away from the epicentre of the madness and consider his options. It was an offer that, he wrote, 'didn't fit in with my plans at the time – I just wanted to get back to playing football as quickly as possible'.

After breaking his arm while elbowing George Boateng in the head during a 4-0 defeat to Aston Villa earlier that season, his time on Teesside was over by 2000. As well as his self-inflicted injury, he received a three-match ban and a £5,000 fine from the FA. It was a warning sign of a declining man as well as a declining footballer. Released on a free, he begged Walter Smith for a move to Everton, pleading 'Please, Walter. Will you help me? Take me back?' Smith gave him a two-year contract, but, although he started the season well, recurring injuries and his mental state meant that by Christmas he was out of the side. 'Football is all I know, all I've ever known,' he admitted, 'so being out of it was utter misery. I drank to pass the time, to make the days go quickly. That was the point of drinking.'

The former Rangers manager wanted Gascoigne to go to a clinic but the player was determined that he would not do it. 'Please, please – anything but that,' he implored. 'A month out of football, while the season is still going on, will destroy me. The only thing that makes my life worth living is football. I can't do it.' Smith told him, 'If you respect me, you will go to the clinic. If not, we'll shake hands now and you can walk away from Everton.' The management convinced him to go to a clinic in Arizona called Cottonwood. Gascoigne stayed away from a drink for another nine months. When he returned to Cottonwood for a second time, he took it more seriously. He had been a stranger in the US, which was better for him. Nobody knew him as 'Gazza'. Nobody knew him at all, in fact. During the sober period in which he wrote his autobiography, he explained that he 'never actually liked drinking', only doing it to 'numb my brain'. When pondering why he was like he was, he was unsure: 'Fuck knows. Perhaps it's the traumas I've been through …'

Gascoigne had been sober for a year when the first edition of that book came out, but heartbreakingly wrote that, 'I'd like it all to be over, to be in heaven.' Elsewhere in its pages, he reflected, 'I'd like to be a child again. I want to be seven …' and of his hope that he would die before his parents do. He could not live with alcohol, but neither could he live (happily) without it. Looking back on his playing career, he realised that through injury and addiction, his achievements in football were limited. 'Let's say I fulfilled my dreams,' he wrote, 'but I didn't fulfil my potential.' We know now that he would eventually drink again, with predictable results, but Gascoigne pondered 'whether I'll keep this up. I haven't done in the past, so everyone thinks it won't last this time.'

❧❧❧

It's sometimes said that if Gascoigne had been given a make-work job, 'something to do', after he had quit playing, that things would have been different. This neglects to recognise that his problems were already well underway by this point, but perhaps more importantly it is another strain of the wishful thinking that comes with 'doing a geographical'. Which is to say, the attempts alcoholics make to alter their lives, perhaps even the way they drink, by planning elaborate moves which may – or may not – eventually occur. The thinking seems to go that 'If I wasn't around these people, with all the ways they annoy me, or encourage me to drink, or otherwise affect my life, I would drink sensibly and there would be nothing to worry about.'

For Gascoigne, it suggests that if he was occupied by something, he would drink normally, or at least close to it, because he would not have the time to drink alcoholically. This seems like woolly thinking, because it supposes that he would not have made time for drinking, crafting a situation so that he could pursue the beers too, as he had done while he was playing. Indeed, during a spell in charge of Kettering Town, this proved to be the case. Sure, a job within the structure of a big club under a manager he was close with might have slowed the process but the trajectory would have been the same because it put the cart before the horse. A job in football would have been great for Gascoigne if it had followed a period of sobriety and was the foundation of a new life. But it could not be the cure in and of itself, because he was taking 'Gascoigne the Untreated Alcoholic' into it.

II
SATURDAY NIGHTS AND
SUNDAY MORNINGS

6.

LIFE'S A FUNNY OLD GAME

'All I know is that the years from '74 to '78
were lost to me' – Jimmy Greaves

HERE is the story of Hughie Gallacher. A Scotsman, from Belshill to be precise, who got his big footballing break in the 1920s. Married to his childhood sweetheart Annie McIlvaney when he was aged just 17, he fathered a son who died before his first birthday. The marriage did not last, and although another child followed they eventually separated for good. Making his name at Queen of the South and then Airdrie, he had arrived at Newcastle United in 1926, where he met his second wife.

They would eventually marry when he was a Chelsea player, and west London was a prime location for his full-on lifestyle. Gallacher became a fixture on the social scene and one or two nocturnal incidents were cause for Chelsea to drop him periodically. 'I was fond of a drink,' he said, but his team-mate Dick Spence recalled, 'I never knew it to affect his performance on the field.' As is so often the case, it was the hangers-on who were seen as the problem; he could not say no and it seems that this bustling area of London was not, in some respects, the best place for him.

He was a short-tempered man – on the pitch too – and served several two-month suspensions imposed by the FA. When Newcastle played a game in Hungary, the entire team had been accused of being drunk on the pitch and threatened with having their match fee withheld by the Hungarian footballing authorities. The explanation was that, in the hot weather, they had washed their mouths out with whisky before taking the field, and the smell had remained on their breath. The FA sided with them but, as Gallacher said, 'Once again my hasty tongue has got me into trouble.' When he was finally granted a divorce from his first wife six years on, he had debts amounting to £787, a staggering sum in the 1930s. Eventually, he was transferred to Derby and it was arranged for his debts to be discharged upon payment of a £200 fee.

After football, Gallacher considered becoming a publican, but his second wife, perhaps wisely, thought better of it. When she died as a result of a heart condition, he began to drink even more. He was quite clearly in trouble at this point. 'Drink has been my downfall,' he said. In 1957 his 14-year-old son was taken into care following suspicions of neglect and abuse on Gallacher's part and court proceedings were set into motion. Gallacher could not take it and headed for a railway line near Low Fell station near his home in Gateshead. An ex-manager from his playing days saw him crossing a footbridge, unaware of what was about to happen.

Gallacher said 'sorry' then jumped in front of an Edinburgh-bound express train at 12.08pm on 11 June 1957. He died, aged 54. Later, a message was found reading, 'It's no good fighting this thing now.'

✵✵✵

The tale of Gallacher's demise was a cautionary one for our next subject who, like him, had a spell at Chelsea. For the aforementioned Scotsman, the burden of his affliction was too much and he saw only one way out, yet for Jimmy Greaves, to whom we move now, there was another option: the rooms of Alcoholics Anonymous. His path there was, by definition, a rocky one, but when he chose to avail himself of that fork in the road, he began a sunnier new chapter.

There is a commonly held misconception that Greaves's ill-fated transfer to Milan in 1961 or his exclusion from the final of the 1966 World Cup were what tipped him into an alcoholic spiral (although he only made three appearances for his national side after that defining tournament). 'I was pleased we'd won,' he said, 'but inside I just felt numb.'

After he had reluctantly agreed a transfer to AC Milan, Greaves missed his scheduled flight to the Italian city. He had been imbibing with a friendly *Express* journalist in the airport, but caught another plane six hours later and went on to score in a 2-2 draw in a friendly the next day. It was, as with the World Cup several years later, a formative experience. He wrote that 'traps had been set' as far as his later relationship with drinking was concerned. The alcoholic phase would come later, beginning when he was a West Ham player. Yet his experiences of being transferred against his own better judgement marked the point when he realised that he could use alcohol to change how he felt and transport himself to a 'false world'. Neither was he a saint, even before the drink took hold. In the months before the 1966 World Cup, he and his England team-mates had snuck out of their hotel to go to the Beachcomber for a drink or two. When they returned, Alf Ramsey had placed the passports of each culprit on their pillow, his own quiet gesture to let them know that he knew what they had been up to.

The following day he had made his feelings clearer, telling the squad, 'You may all go and get changed now, except, that is, those players who I believe would like to stay and talk with me.' When innocent parties had peeled away, he informed the remnant, 'You can count yourself lucky. If there had been enough players in this squad, I would have sent you all home when back in London. Gentlemen, may I for the first and last time remind you of your responsibilities as members of the England team. All I hope is that you have learned your lesson and will not behave in such an irrational and irresponsible manner again. Gentlemen, the matter is now closed.'

When they beat Portugal 4-3, two of the escapee drinkers scored. Now, Ramsey was willing to permit a small tipple, 'Gentlemen, you may now partake of a beer if you are so inclined. Jimmy and Bobby, I'll have a gin and tonic …' he told them. On another occasion, a request was made by a few players to go for a drink before returning to their hotel. 'We shall go back to the hotel *together*,' he told them.

He rarely swore but saw fit to this time, adding: 'If you want a fucking beer you come back to the hotel and have it.'

Greaves's drinking did not cause any concerns at this point. Looking back, though, he reflected on how he 'enjoyed becoming an alcoholic', and that heavy-drinking team-mates were 'not necessarily alcoholics' because, quite simply, they knew when they had had enough. At Tottenham, the team would regularly debrief about that weekend's performance at the White Hart or the Bell and Hare. Bill Nicholson was happy enough with this arrangement 'as long as we were giving 110 per cent on the pitch and in training'. Greaves added, 'Even now I would not discourage young footballers from having this sort of after-match wind-down session. But I would advise them to pack up and go home after a couple of pints.'

Another managerial intervention some years later would leave a particularly sour taste in Greaves's mouth. It was four years later, during the 1970/71 season, and West Ham were due to play Blackpool. Heavy snow had cast the fixture into extreme doubt, to the extent that the squad were convinced it would be postponed. West Ham had been something of a boozy club during the 1960s with Bobby Moore, John Cushley, Brian Dear, Frank Lampard, John Charles, Harry Redknapp, Jimmy Lindsay and sometimes Geoff Hurst among those partaking in their nights out. Moore and Martin Peters had even recorded a television ad for their local pub. It was perhaps unsurprising, then, that when a surplus taxi arrived at their hotel the night before the match, several players took the opportunity to head into a city-centre bar, not returning to their base until 1.45am.

Greaves had put away 12 lagers on his own. Bobby Moore and Brian Dear had had half a dozen each. Clyde Best consumed one measly soft drink. When they awoke at 10am, the players still believed the match would not go ahead that day. When it did, the visitors in claret and blue lost 4-0. Their secret was safe for another 36 hours, until one of their own supporters grassed them up to a newspaper. The players in question were fined and dropped, a move which was to be expected in the circumstances. What upset them was that it was carried out in public and any respect Greaves had had for their manager Ron Greenwood disappeared. It was Bobby Moore's first indiscretion in 15 years at the club. Yet Greaves saw his friend being 'hung out to dry', believing it to be a deflating moment for his team-mate. 'I was,' he wrote, 'particularly nauseated by the treatment [he] got.'

By now, Greaves was using drink as a way of coping with life. But it was this incident that convinced him he should hang up his boots before too long. 'I knew every pub from Aldgate Pump to Southend,' he wrote. By May of 1971 he had left West Ham and, in doing so, professional football. There had been talk of a move to Brian Clough's Derby. He had played alongside Ol' Big 'Ead for England twice in 1959 – Clough's only appearances for his nation – but the transfer talk came to nothing.

His full-time football career was over. For the next two years, Greaves did not touch a football or even attend a match, such was his disillusionment with the game. The next five years, unchained from the daily discipline that football had provided, led to the breakdown of his marriage.

He was aged 31 when he quit professional football and some people, not least his wife, thought he had given up too soon. Instead, he drank. Every day. Typically, that would consist of up to 16 pints of beer, topped up by eight short drinks. He had enough money to carry on this way and the first two years he just about managed to hold it all together. 'People close to me,' he wrote, 'knew I had a problem but it was not generally well known in the football world.'

Predictably, things soon fell apart. He began drinking every hour that he was awake, stashing – as many alcoholics do – vodka around the house to guzzle at stolen moments away from prying eyes. Some days he would put away 20 pints, always ensuring one of those bottles of vodka was by his bed to help him through those first few minutes awake. Some days he would drink Guinness, or, as he called it, 'my only food of the day'. Had football's culture in the 1960s played a role in his predicament, even if it was not responsible for his alcoholism on its own? He thought so: players had a lot of time to themselves after training, with few of the commitments that even relatively obscure players would have today. He tried playing football, which he so missed, at a lower level. But it was difficult to take it seriously and derive the same thrill from it. Seeing parallels in his own life with the former Chelsea and Newcastle forward Hughie Gallacher, he would always stand at the back of railway platforms.

Periodically, he would admit himself to a private nursing home for 'rest and supervision', typically checking in after an especially long and heavy bout of drinking. By now he was fully aware of his alcoholism, plain even to him after he had been through the bins to find bottles his wife had discarded in desperation the previous evening. One doctor put him in touch with Alcoholics Anonymous, but he was not ready to listen, not believing he was at – or would reach – the level of the people he heard there. After a while, he left the family home, setting up in a bedsit in Wanstead.

Finally, he phoned AA again, realising the scale of his predicament. This time, he took their words on board. It was not easy: he would try to get through an hour at a time, then a day, still craving the temporary release that alcohol could bring. Those weeks became months and then a year. His separation from his wife had become a divorce, but he renewed contact with Eileen and their children once again. Continuing his attendance at AA meetings, he wrote, 'I rediscovered the feeling of love, compassion and companionship.' He gratefully explained that they had 'saved me from drinking myself to death'.

He learned what he labels the 'three As' – admission, adjustment, achievement – and described himself as 'evangelical' about its programme, advocating that the 500,000 people in the UK thought to be alcoholics at that time should give it a shot. A definitive measure of who is an alcoholic is difficult to make – one person's heavy drinker is another's alcoholic – so estimates of alcoholism in England range from between one and ten per cent of the population depending on where the boundary is drawn. Beyond this, it is a factor in all four of the major causes of death for men aged between 20 and 40: suicide, accidents, homicide and cirrhosis of the liver. In 1994, 15 years after Greaves's 'coming out', one in ten men and one in 20 women were said to have a drink problem. More than a quarter of the population were drinking beyond the weekly recommended limit of 21 units and, by their own admission, around half were drinking more than the 'safe' level. The charity Alcohol Concern classed one in 20 as being an alcoholic.

Royalties from his first autobiography, which detailed this episode in his life, *This One's On Me*, went to pay off his debt to the taxman. When Greaves took up football again, it was for non-league Barnet in the Southern League. 'I was of the mind that the more interests I had,' he wrote, 'the less chance there was of my mind dwelling on booze.' He described his time there elsewhere as a 'release valve', saying, 'Now I am leaning heavily on football to help me through my crisis.'

Despite the relatively small crowds, the return to football helped him. 'I was back playing football and enjoying it,' he said. Taking up a midfield role to compensate for his understandable loss of pace, he received understanding from the club if he was absent from training if he needed to stay in the safety of his flat or visit an AA meeting. Even the quips he received from the crowd were good-humoured, gentle barbs such as 'Mind you don't hit the bar, Greavsie.' During the 1978/79 season, when Barry Fry was in charge, he decided it was time to hang up those boots for good. He was ready to take on new things, and wrote, 'I could see light at the end of the tunnel and for once it wasn't a train coming.' It would grant him more time to see his ex-wife and children, from whom he still lived apart. Though their divorce became absolute in 1979, the prospects of an eventual reconciliation were promising.

In an interview that year on London Weekend Television's *Russell Harty Plus* show, Greaves spoke of his alcoholism, conceding that although he would always be one, 'I must be a non-drinking alcoholic.' It was a broadcast that, in 1979, was seen as a landmark since Greaves was the first high-profile footballer to make such an admission. He knew he had an -ism and was only too aware that 'unfortunately it never becomes a "wasm"'. Months later Eileen indicated she was ready to give her ex-husband another try. He returned to the family home. 'That night,' he wrote, 'as I made my way back to my flat for the very last time, I had tears of joy in my eyes.' For the man who now described himself as a 'screenaholic', a second television appearance in a documentary about his alcoholism and recovery titled *Just For Today* was his route into the broadcasting career for which he is fondly remembered.

⚜

Though the arc of his story was redemptive, Greaves stated that his 'real drinking' started after he had quit the game. 'In my frustration at having let the good times go,' he said, 'I turned to the bottle.' Once retired, players without a plan are on a road to nowhere. They have made more money than their school friends would in dozens of lifetimes and will never again take to the field at Old Trafford, the Emirates, the Bernabeu or Camp Nou. In 1985 the average yearly salary of a top-flight player was £25,000, already 250 per cent more than the average man on the street. Today, their earnings will be 35 times more than someone doing a regular job. It would be easy for them to think that their best years had been and gone; that everything will be a disappointment from now on. For many, the adjustment process will lead them to ruin, personally and often financially. Gone are the routines of several training sessions a week, club staff to call on and the regular adrenaline rush of matches twice a week. For those who relished being recognised – perhaps despite their protestations otherwise – the end of their playing days may signpost a slow slide into relative obscurity that will, for some, be hard to take.

Tommy Caton was a centre-back who had started his career as an apprentice at Manchester City. After a fitful spell at Arsenal, he spent a year at Oxford United before being sold to Charlton Athletic for £100,000 in order to continue appearing in the First Division. When Charlton were relegated at the end of the 1989/90 season, he stuck with them in the second tier but, after injuring his right ankle in January 1991, Caton never played again. Injuries, especially those persisting for more than three or four weeks, will often see a player fall into some form of low mood or even into depression. His contract was finally cancelled in March 1993, just a month before his death from a heart attack.

His star never shone as brightly as it had at City. There, he was considered a teenage sensation and became the youngest player to achieve 100 appearances during the 1982/83 campaign, hitting 198 by the time he was 21. Two games short of his double century, he left City for what he hoped would be a more stable situation at Arsenal in the wake of managerial turmoil at Maine Road. It was not to be. He cycled through four managers at Highbury, eventually losing his place to Martin Keown, and by 1987 the emergence of David O'Leary into the first team put an end to any hopes of re-establishing himself in the side.

Though his career had ebbed by the turn of the decade, he had played 57 times for Charlton, scoring five goals in the process. He had never entirely fulfilled what his early career had promised but in that he is not unique. The tragic aspect of Caton's story comes with his injury. Though the cause of death was cardiac arrest, the defender had effectively drank himself to death. Three children had lost their father, his wife Gill a husband. She reported that he had been drinking two bottles of gin a day in the two years since he had last played because 'he didn't think he could do anything outside playing football'. He had died the day before Brian Clough's last home game as manager of Nottingham Forest.

The lessons of Greaves and Caton support research which suggests that the most dangerous time for a player's mental health is just after retirement. Those defining few weeks after they have hung up their boots can set the stage for what follows. That is when their difficulties are most likely to bubble to the surface and the conditions that the player has been suppressing throughout his career are now free to flourish; anxiety and depression, a smoking habit, bad sleep, unusual eating routines and what the academics Gouttebarge, Aoki and Kerkhoffs call 'adverse alcohol behaviour'.

Given the loss of status, identity and routine, it is little wonder that a FIFPro publication found that 35 per cent of retired players reported having depression or anxiety, often presenting within the first few weeks of them hanging up their boots. The equivalent figure for the general population is less than half that. This is to be expected: for people in regular forms of employment, the majority will have done their adjusting to life's challenges in their late adolescence and have a pretty good idea about who they are by the time they reach their mid-30s. In many cases, football players are undergoing that process of self-discovery at twice the age of their non-footballing peers and some will turn to self-medicating to try and fix the way they feel: a staggering one in four retired players were found to self-report 'adverse' behaviour of this kind.

When 229 retired players were surveyed, three-quarters responded that they were in full-time employment of some description at the time of answering. Generally, the symptoms being looked for are most common in young adults than anyone else and would tend to lessen as an individual gets older, learning coping mechanisms or simply 'growing out' of such behaviours. Yet these randomly selected retired players had a higher incidence of all of these, more so than still active players or members of the general population. Only four per cent of active players report 'adverse behaviour' in relation to smoking compared to nearly 12 per cent who have put their feet up and nine per cent among active players in terms of adverse alcohol behaviour as opposed to 25 per cent in the retired cohort.

The category of 'professional footballer' is one recognised by both the World Health Organisation and the International Labour Organisation as a distinct entity. As a result, clubs, as employers, have a lifelong obligation to the wellbeing of their players. But this is not a responsibility that appears to be fulfilled as diligently as it could be. The same of which can be said of the footballing authorities. Given the amount of money at the top level of the game, it seems troubling that this is not a commitment they feel able to honour, particularly in the crucial few months shortly after a player has retired.

7.

LEAD HIM TO WATER

'A manager cannot be responsible
for his players 24 hours of the day' –
George Graham

'I can't live with him 24 hours a day' –
Matt Busby on George Best

TONY Adams knew full well that if Gareth Southgate missed *that* penalty at Wembley on 26 June 1996, he would be getting drunk. He had 'white-knuckled' it through the preceding weeks while his team-mates partied in the dentist's chair, all too aware that one drink would have set him off down a road with no room for a quick u-turn.

'I knew if I went with them, I would be on the piss and gone. The tournament would be gone for me,' he wrote later, referencing the boisterous high jinks of his compatriots on their Far East jaunt. 'It's the first time in my life,' he said, 'that I didn't want to drink but I was still getting drunk. It frightened the life out of me. I couldn't control this anymore.'

Adams had captained the side through friendlies in the preceding years, after Terry Venables had entrusted him with the armband in October 1994 – shortly after his 28th birthday – in a match versus Romania. The press, perhaps understandably, had worried about the wisdom of awarding the captaincy to a man with a drink-driving conviction. He had met with Venables at Scott's in Mayfair so the manager could explain how he saw the team shaping up. On that occasion, Adams drank three-quarters of the two bottles of wine they shared over the dinner table. It was the start of a three-day bender, which was not uncommon for the defender back then. There had been that time with Niall Quinn, with whom he often drank in Irish bars around Camden, shortly before Arsenal's title-deciding match against Liverpool in 1989. There was also the time he had fallen paralytic down the stairs of a nightclub and required 29 stitches; or the time he had spent nearly two months in prison after driving his car drunk. You get the picture.

When Adams was picked up by the police in 1990 for drink-driving, he registered a .134 blood alcohol level on the breathalyser. When he was tested for a second time, at which point you might have expected the alcohol level to have decreased, it registered .137. Unsurprisingly, he was arrested. That December he was sentenced to four months in jail and, where leniency had been expected, it was denied. There was a high-profile anti-drink-driving campaign being broadcast and it may have been efficacious to make an example of a high-profile sportsman. As he waited to go down to the cells, Adams was handcuffed to another inbound prisoner, who remarked, 'This has really capped my day. I'm a Tottenham fan and I get cuffed to you.'

In his cell, said to be where the interior shots from *Porridge* were filmed, Adams could have got hold of a small amount of alcohol to consume surreptitiously, but instead he thought 'there was no point in having such a small amount. I would rather have nothing.' He was offered the opportunity to see out much of his sentence in Ford Open Prison in West Sussex but opted to stay put; he felt safe where he was and had found his niche advising the prison side ahead of a match against the Essex Police force. He received visits and letters from Arsenal team-mates, mostly reminding him it would not be long before he was out and other good wishes. One letter from one Arsenal peer did surprise him, however, 'by pointing out forcefully that I had done wrong'.

When Adams was released, he knew that even though his return to drinking was not immediate, it would happen eventually. Losing his liberty was not enough to permanently terrify him out of something so deeply, ritualistically ingrained in his life. His first fixture after being released was for Arsenal's reserves, against Reading, which attracted a crowd of in excess of 7,000 fans to watch their formerly imprisoned centre-back. No longer able to drive himself around, he turned to Ray Parlour, fulfilling his duties in a Mini Metro. Often, they would head into central London after training for a 'quick one', only to emerge hours later the worse for wear, ending up leaving the vehicle in the heart of the city for several days.

It's little wonder, then, that he felt the need to lock himself away in his 15th-floor room when England had travelled to Hong Kong. The Arsenal centre-back had proven his fitness in a pre-Euro 96 friendly after injury had laid him low in January, but he was beginning to sense that alcohol was his kryptonite and could do more lasting damage in his life than his knackered knee ever would. After Southgate's soft penalty against the Germans at Wembley, he had 'no mental defence', and, whereas Gascoigne could barely speak in that excruciating moment, Adams headed straight for the crate of beers in the changing room, barely pausing for breath throughout the next seven weeks.

His first proper drinking experience had come a year after signing professional terms with Arsenal. Adams had injured his foot playing for the reserves, disrupting his usual footballing routine and giving him time to indulge. It was the first time that drinking had seemed important. Back then, he was the baby of the group and could still perform well after a heavy night, occasionally putting in man-of-the-match performances while still drunk from the night before. At that time, he was the club's second-youngest debutant when he made his appearance versus Sunderland in November 1983. It was all a long way from the wet beds, soiled mattresses and hallucinations that would follow.

'But Gareth, it was a shit penalty wasn't it?' he had teased Southgate later that night in London in 1996, exaggeratedly booing his team-mate as he came into the bar later before their final night at Burnham Beeches. The next morning, he would try to persuade Southgate and Pearce to have one more pint with him before they went their separate ways. They declined his offer. But for Adams it was not that simple. 'Once I started drinking,' he wrote, 'I had to carry on until I was drunk.'

There would, in the short term, be no stopping him. He knew that it was going to be a big one. When he was in the pub, Adams described himself as 'like a kid at the pick 'n' mix sweet counter' surveilling the pumps and their assorted offerings. There was one thing that helped to curb some of his worst excesses on the drink. 'When I had my football,' he said, 'I was all right.' Yet, at other moments he would wonder, 'Why can't you stop this, now?' Football itself would also provide a framework for Adams's drinking, too: 'Drink and football,' he wrote, 'my two saviours.' There were regular Saturday night sessions, part of the life of a professional footballer in the late 80s and early 90s. Wednesday night sessions were more than possible too, with British teams banned from European competition after the Heysel disaster in 1985.

Then there was the Tuesday Club. That was the name of Arsenal's famous drinking society of that era, although the club had a reputation as a boozy one even during the 1970s. Perry Groves, a contemporary of Adams at the height of George Graham's reign at Highbury, recalled: 'Training ended early on Tuesday afternoon. Then we could do what we wanted until Thursday morning, when we had to report back. It turned into a mammoth drinking session. It was usually an all-day bender. Most of the players went along – even the married ones would stay for most of the day. At that time, it was the done thing in the game. You'd go out, and you'd bump into lads from Charlton or QPR or

Chelsea, whoever.' The players would train at Highbury on Tuesdays, one of George Graham's tough, physical sessions without the ball. That morning, they would arrive with smarter clothes to change into, in order to aid a quick transition from training to the more carefree type of session which followed. Most often, this was in Islington or Covent Garden.

Langan's in Mayfair was another familiar haunt and George Graham would send his assistant Stewart Houston out on reconnaissance missions to ascertain what his players were up to. On one occasion, they were spotted at Champions in Southgate on a day when a number of the party were due to play in a reserve match later that day. Those players snuck out the back of the establishment as Houston chatted with the players not encumbered by this responsibility.

While making a name for himself at the club, Adams looked to Graham Rix and Kenny Sansom for drinking advice. The former told him to 'drink Guinness' due to its fast-acting properties. It would go on to become a favourite intoxicant for Adams, who could, in his drinking stride, consume 'about four pints an hour'. Sansom, of course, would face his own very public, ongoing battle with the bottle. On Sundays, almost without fail, they would go to the Chequers, where Adams operated a fine-based system for early departures and other perceived infringements of the group's rules. On one occasion, Adams left the pub with little warning during the middle of the afternoon, only to be spotted on the television later – slightly worse for wear – picking out one half of the FA Cup draw. When he returned, he fined himself £200 and ordered that the rest of the crew should continue drinking until 1am or risk their own financial penalty.

In the latter years of his drinking, Adams would put on a bin-liner when he trained to sweat out the booze, but when the Sunday sessions started to get out of control, he was 'turning up pissed' to Monday morning training sessions after a heavy weekend. He told himself that he could not be an alcoholic because he refrained from drinking on a Friday night. 'If I was that good on the pitch, I couldn't be that bad off it, could I?' he asked rhetorically. Yet beneath the bravado on the surface, he was falling apart. When he found himself a single man again after the disintegration of his first marriage, he would barely be able to manage a shower before heading out drinking once more.

Though it may have been easier to evade getting caught out back then, Graham did have rules, but they were enforced only sporadically. As Perry Groves noted, 'George turned a blind eye to it. The fact was that as long as you were doing it for him on the pitch, he didn't care. It only became a problem if you weren't doing it for him. And in Tony Adams's case, he was putting in great performances for the club every week.' Ray Parlour recalled an incident involving the discharging of a fire extinguisher by Adams in a Pizza Hut, for which Parlour (the younger man) was fined two weeks' wages while Adams inexplicably escaped without punishment.

Parlour himself fell foul of the law in Hong Kong on another occasion as a result of his drunken rowdiness, leading *The Mirror* to fume that he had 'shamed the nation'.

Though the justice system had levied just a small fine upon him, the club had a public relations battle to fight. Peter Hill-Wood, Arsenal chairman between 1982 and 2013, proclaimed 'Football and Arsenal need this like a hole in the head.' He continued: 'When will footballers learn? He has let down not only his team-mates and the club but England as a nation. It was foolish behaviour.' Parlour, aged 22, was fined two weeks' wages and may have still felt he had gotten off lightly were it not for the fact that Arsenal made him pay £12,000 for the barrister's services, which ate up nearly all of the signing-on fee of the new contract he would soon be signing. Years later, Ken Friar (a managing director at the club) told him the club had wanted to teach him a lesson. Fines, and the power to suspend, had been a right clubs had been granted by the league in 1923.

Adams had replaced Sansom as captain after the latter's bust-up with Graham and led the team to the title in 1989, a title decided on the final day of the season against Liverpool, who were their direct rivals for the crown. Yet he confessed to feeling 'empty' after their triumph, strolling up to a locked Highbury around 7am on Sunday after an all-nighter. He was spotted drinking from cans of Heineken and Red Stripe on the victory parade later that day. Later, he would admit that 'getting drunk was my way of dealing with the high points as well'.

Seven years later, England's Euro 96 was drifting into his rear-view mirror. Adams was facing time on the sidelines again in order to properly deal with the knee injury that had nearly ruled him out of the tournament. He was off the leash: his marriage to his wife, Jane, had begun to crumble earlier in the year as she sought help for her own addictions. Obligations at home would not be keeping him from bars around London's West End. This would go on until the early evening of Friday, 16 August 1996 when, at around five in the evening, Adams took his last drink from that day to now.

Though it was the end of another binge that had begun at the start of that week, it was, in reality, the culmination of 12 years of drinking. Blackouts – wondering where he had been, what had gone on, if he had disgraced himself – had become the norm. When the fear had set in, he had dealt with it by drinking more, and once he started again he could not stop until he passed out. That night he took himself home via the fish and chip shop, knowing that he did not want to repeat this cycle any more. There were tears, of remorse, of frustration, of relief, and also sadness at the likely closing of a chapter of his life that Friday night represented.

Adams locked himself away at home that weekend in bed, sweating out the booze, hungover and dealing with the inevitable withdrawal symptoms that follow the sudden cessation of drinking after a prolonged bout. When Monday finally arrived, he took himself to Arsenal's training facility at Shenley Sports grounds and told Arsenal's Steve Jacobs, a recovering gambling addict and player-whisperer at the club, 'I've got a drink problem and I need to go to a meeting of Alcoholics Anonymous.'

It had been during the 1993/94 season that Adams had first noticed his off-field behaviour affecting his game. Before a match against Everton, he realised that his drinking over the previous days meant that he would not be able to perform anywhere near his best. Yet his pride would not let him miss the game. Instead, he told George Graham, from the screaming-and-shouting school of management, that he was ill but would play anyway. When he was substituted, Graham thanked him for trying despite his ailment. Adams had manipulated the situation in order that his own lack of professionalism inadvertently reflected positively on him.

The problem that Graham had was that Adams, and Paul Merson, were two of the best players in his Arsenal squad alongside Ian Wright. He took a hard line on other players for minor infractions but was unable to impose similar iron discipline upon the 'Sons of George' because they were integral to any success the team would have. If they had been past their prime or putting in consistently bad performances, he may have been able to justify shipping them out. This allowed a culture to develop at Arsenal – one that included the half-time routine during which captain Adams would motivate the drinkers in the side by reminding them that they were only 45 minutes from being able to get on the beers. As Adams would later realise, 'Football had become irrelevant to me.' Indeed, his own father had told him, 'You don't smile anymore when you play.'

After attending a second meeting of Alcoholics Anonymous, Adams felt he belonged and, owing to his knee injury, had the time to throw himself into going to meetings in the same way he had dedicated himself to drinking for the previous decade or so. In fact, he estimated that he went along to 100 such meetings in the first 90 days that he was sober. On Friday, 13 September 1996 – four weeks after that last drink – Adams sat his team-mates down to tell them about the changes that he had made in his life. Looking back at that moment, he reflected, 'Some of the boys may not have thought I was an alcoholic, like other people close to me, but the important thing was that I knew I was.' Ian Wright told him, 'I always thought you had bottle. Now I know.' After his conversation with Steve Jacobs, Adams had attended his first meeting of Alcoholics Anonymous in Fulham. By his own admission, it did not immediately change his life; he had been self-conscious and had not been able to pick up on much of what was going on.

❧❧

Alcoholics Anonymous had its genesis 61 years earlier, on 10 June 1935. That was the day when one of its founders, Robert 'Doctor Bob' Smith, took his last drink. Dr Bob was a surgeon from Akron, Ohio, who had, from his late teens, struggled to reliably stay away from the bottle. By 1935 Bob was in his early 50s and despite his – and his wife's – best efforts, he had fallen under the influence once again. In May he met Bill Wilson – sometimes referred to as Bill W – who was a Wall Street trader. A month later Bob would take the last drink of his life and the two men would go on to usher Alcoholics Anonymous into existence with the goal of helping people like them to help themselves through their common purpose and mutual aid. Four years after its founding, this new 'fellowship' published *Alcoholics Anonymous*, commonly known as the Big Book, which they saw as a 'spiritual toolkit' for the newly (and not so newly) sober man and woman. Fundamentally, they saw alcoholics as being 'bodily different' from the non-addicted people, believing their brains simply deal with the ingestion of alcoholic substances in their own way. This thinking aligns with the disease model of alcoholism – that the brains of addicts actually do light up in different ways to those of others and respond to different stimuli.

❦

The following week, Adams had gone along to another meeting in St Albans with Paul Merson, and his Arsenal and England team-mate told him, 'You were nodding like one of those toy dogs.' This time, the meeting made an impact. Weeks later, when he opened up to his Arsenal team-mates, Andy Linighan had told him, 'You've cracked it Tone, you've taken the first step.' For others in the dressing room, it would be a moment of reflection. In his autobiography, Ray Parlour writes of how he had privately thought, 'Some of us drink more than you, Tone.' Indeed, he goes on, 'If he was an alcoholic, perhaps that meant we must be alcoholics as well,' although he clarified that 'I always thought Tony was more of a binge drinker to be honest.' Patrick Vieira, who had only arrived at the club 30 days earlier, did not understand very much of Adams's speech (he had not learned much English then) but realised he 'must have come to the right place if a man – the captain – could stand up in front of his friends and tell them about something like this and moreover if these people could then help him through his problems'.

In the months after finding sobriety, Adams confided in Merson that he had thought his team-mate was 'a bit of an arsehole, but I can see now what you were about'. His friend, in turn, informed him, 'There's a difference between honesty and brutal frankness.' Adams had embraced his new life with the zeal that only a new convert could muster and became frustrated that some of his team-mates could not grasp some of the concepts he was beginning to wrestle with until a friend counselled him, 'Tony, you didn't understand any of this for years. How can you expect them to?'

'People seem to think that once you stop drinking, all your troubles stop,' he wrote. They do not, of course, and Adams went to many meetings in those early days, even when the team was playing abroad. Sometimes he would struggle to sleep, a common affliction in the newly sober, often compounded by the extraordinary amounts of coffee consumed. The club even gave Adams dispensation to miss training when he felt that tending to his emotional and spiritual wellbeing was more important that day. It had finally become clear that he was a 'sick man trying to get well, not a bad man … trying to get good'. The apparently extreme lengths – such as going to meetings after matches – that he was going to in those early days after putting the bottle down baffled one or two of his playing colleagues. He had told Parlour, 'Ray, I really enjoy going out with you, but if you're going out don't phone me up.' They remained roommates on the road and still travelled to training together, but the constant trips to the pub were a thing of the past.

This, coupled with Arsène Wenger's imminent arrival, undoubtedly benefitted Parlour's own career, which could have taken a very different path. For Adams and Merson, already forging a dramatically divergent route from the 90s footballing archetype, Wenger's arrival meant regular 'long walks' with the manager round the training ground as they grew into more reflective characters. Adams would later speak of spending a lot of time with Merson, which had the effect of 'holding up a mirror to a lot of people and reactions were mixed'.

Why had it taken so long? Adams's alcoholism was one of the worst-kept secrets not just in London, but in football itself. It was obvious to his nearest and dearest, but even time spent at Her Majesty's pleasure in Chelmsford prison for a drink-driving offence had failed to provide the wake-up call that he needed to set him on a straighter and narrower path. 'I drank because I was frightened,' Adams wrote, 'and I was frightened because I drank. I couldn't tell which came first.'

It may well have been that for him, as is the case with many alcoholics, being frightened led to getting drunk; a form of escapism from that gnawing feeling of anxiety. The footballer talks of experiencing panic attacks when he was aged 11 or 12, of having an obsessive personality even before he had tasted that first drop of alcohol. When he did, he drank it for its effect, not the way it tasted; a tale similar to that of many – though by no means all – ex-drinkers. But alcohol brought out a destructive side: those terrifying lost afternoons and nights. As Adams puts it, the feeling of, 'Where am I? What happened? What did I say? Have I embarrassed myself, as I have done so many times in the past? How do I get home?'

For the alcoholic, drink is a symptom of their inability to deal with the everyday things of life in the way that their unaddicted peers are able to. When Adams awoke with the fear the next day, he would, like many others, simply drink more to bury those nagging questions. As he acknowledged later, 'Drinking, when I got the chance between games, was helping me to cope with it all, I thought.'

After finding sobriety, Adams conducted himself differently on and around the field of play as well as off it. During a match versus Derby he was given a red card, and with Merson having already departed the field injured they went to the players' lounge for a cup of tea rather than sit and stew on the sidelines. Once upon a time it would have been straight to the crate in the dressing room and angry talk of recriminations. In fact, Adams would go on to suggest closing the players' bar for one trial season – including the cessation of drinking on the coach home from away games – and, with the broad consensus of his Arsenal team-mates, it was enacted. It was all a long way from the days when Adams was turning out for England alongside Terry Butcher, whose mantra was 'win or lose, we will booze'.

In the 1997/98 season, Adams's first full term after kicking the bottle, Arsenal won the league and cup double. It was Arsène Wenger's first complete term in the hot seat and Adams told his manager, 'You have the best of Tony Adams.' He had come back into the team at the end of September 1996, six weeks after that painful Friday evening and two weeks since he had told the dressing room about the change he had initiated in his life. Not that all of them had realised that there was a need for such a radical departure from his old ways. Paul Davis recalled, 'I don't honestly think that anyone was really aware. We all knew that Tony and Paul liked a drink, but in Tony's case it never appeared to affect his performances.' In 2002, when Adams retired, Wenger told him, 'I cannot believe how you achieved everything you have with the way you abused your body and mind. You have played to only 70 per cent of your capacity.'

There was certainly a new seriousness to Adams in sobriety. Yet there was a new curiosity too. The defender wrote of 'bec[oming] obsessive about drawing and painting' in that first month free of booze but still unable to play through injury. He also found himself growing fond of the sitcom *Frasier*, the eponymous lead character of which he felt an identification with. He rented a flat in Hampstead to look 'cool', costing him £27,000 over six months, despite the fact he did not stay there on a single occasion. He smoked, briefly, without ever having done so before, because it was a way to change the way he felt after the option of alcoholic oblivion had been removed.

8.

JUST ABOUT MANAGING

'Was Brian Clough a genius or was he off his head?' – Stan Bowles

'Walk on water? I know most people out there will be saying that instead of walking on it, I should have taken more of it with my drinks. They are absolutely right' – Brian Clough

IT was on 1 May 1993 that Brian Clough took charge of his last home game after 18 years as manager of Nottingham Forest. That day, the words of Barry Davies about the irascible elder statesman of the English game rang out on the commentary: 'The man with the green sweater … Whatever his failings, whatever his foibles, he's been a power of good for the game of football …' Looking much older than his 58 years, the skin on his face was blotchy and his dealings with players and press alike had drifted from comical to concerning.

Clough had been appointed manager in 1975, back when Forest had an electronic scoreboard – courtesy of their sponsors at the Shipstone & Sons brewery – showing its cartoon footballer 'Ivor Thirst'. Forest won promotion to the First Division just two years later, and by 1979 they were European champions. They repeated the feat again the following year and to this day remain the team from the smallest conurbation to become kings of the continent. That magic, however, had very much faded by that spring day in the early 90s. Forest were doomed to almost certain relegation back to the second tier and the result that day against Sheffield United sealed their fate.

The preceding weeks had been consumed by debate about whether Clough's reign would be coming to an end. One question stood out above all: was Clough going of his own volition, or had he been pushed? What was certain was that nobody was happy that it had come to this. The discomfort was only compounded by the fact that Ol' Big 'Ead's 27-year-old son Nigel, a teetotaller who would often act as chauffeur to his team-mates, was a forward in his father's side.

That day Davies asked Clough Jr, 'Is his health good? He doesn't seem to be a well man.' The son rebuffed this nosy inquisition into his dad's medical state, offering that he was not getting any younger and that perhaps the years were taking their toll. Davies probed further, suggesting that 58 was not that old and that some in the football business were worried about his apparent decline.

Weeks earlier a Forest director, Chris Wootton, had been suspended after allegations were levelled that he had staged an underhand campaign against Clough to undermine the manager's position and force the hand of his fellow directors. Wootton had alleged that the manager regularly got legless before lunchtime. 'I want to see the chairman,' Clough had fumed to Ronnie Fenton, his assistant. 'I want the bastard Wootton sorted out – now!'

He continued to rage of how he 'want[ed] that scumbag kicked out of our club'. Wootton refuted the claims that he had been passing insider information to newspapers but later said that Clough's eventual vacating of his post had 'vindicated' his position. 'I thought it best,' he said, 'for the club and Brian himself for him to consider his position. There has been disquiet among the board for some time.' The rest of the board continued to insist that Clough had retained their support and that Wootton's remarks were untrue. Amid accusation and counter-accusation, Clough suggested that he would sue.

Wootton had leaked an outtake for a Shredded Wheat advert with a voiceover by Clough. In the recording he could be heard slurring his words, and at the end of the clip declared, 'I'm fucking sozzled.' The tape itself was ten months old, and was 'loaned' by Wootton to a local journalist who had sold it to *The People*. The following day Clough featured on the front page of *The Sun* under the headline 'I don't have a drink problem.' He claimed to only drink the occasional sherry or white wine and – of reports that he had fallen asleep in a ditch near his house – explained that he often walked to Nigel's house (a six-to seven-mile journey) and that he had decided to have a rest along the way.

In the *Nottingham Evening Post,* he maintained, 'I'm not a boozer. My chairman told me yesterday he was prepared to say anywhere that he has never seen me the worse for booze ... I have the occasional glass of wine with the chairman and my colleagues at the club over lunch. That's it.' One thing was for sure: the tectonic shift it precipitated had been a few years in the offing. During the previous summer of 1992, transfer dealings had been chaotic. Des Walker was sold to Sampdoria but there was a ready-made replacement in the form of Nottingham lad Darren Wassall. Or there was, until Clough rubbed him up the wrong way and he departed too. Teddy Sheringham was also sold to Tottenham for a shade over £2m and, of those who remained, Roy Keane was grabbing headlines for all the wrong reasons. Although not charged, he was arrested at a party, followed by a further incident in a bar in Jersey while travelling with the club.

In the twilight of his term with Forest, the irascibility and brusqueness that is now set in aspic as part of the Cloughie legend were no longer just an outsized persona – a caricature which he certainly played up to – but simply aspects of his personality. He had tried to sign Dean Saunders from Derby in 1991, and amid the negotiation asked Saunders if he liked flowers. The player replied in the affirmative and Clough went into his garden and put together a selection. Saunders joined Liverpool instead. His case, and that of Gary McAllister, demonstrated that Clough was putting off potential signings who were wary of just how odd, and often rude, their prospective manager could be even when he didn't have a drink inside him. His unpredictability was well known by now. He was rumoured to have punched – at various times – Stuart Pearce, Neil Webb, Roy Keane and Nigel Jemson in the stomach. In lighter moments, he might just as soon hug them.

It had not always been like this. In a previous era, Peter Taylor had been in charge of transfers and they would ask potential recruits, 'Let's hear your vice before you sign, is it women, booze, drugs or gambling?' In *With Clough By Taylor*, his assistant wrote: 'Worry off the field shows itself on the field and damages our aim of a maximum performance on match days, so it's a crime against the team to retain a problem.' Taylor would tell newly signed players, 'You must come to us ... we have to know everything.' Clough had his own methods too. 'If someone likes a beer,' he said, 'I'll get close enough to smell his breath in the morning. Now that's management.'

Not that drinking was discouraged by Clough and Taylor. Quite the opposite, in fact. In the week before their first European Cup win, the players were allowed to drink. On the coach to Munich's Olympic Stadium for their match against Malmo, there were a few crates of beer on board which the players were free to sample. Curfews were not imposed, just a warning not to complain of hangovers. When they had defeated Liverpool in the first round on their way to their European triumph, Clough had taken the team to the pub for 'two half pints each' and a game of dominoes the night before the match. Before the return leg, he had ordered Chablis for his players to drink at lunch to aid their ability to nap in preparation for that night's fixture. Clough saw these exercises as a way to loosen his players up, taking their minds off the match and building team spirit through shared experience. 'What's wrong with a beer or two en route to the ground?' he asked.

When one player was offered a drink shortly before another game, he declined, telling Clough that he hoped he would be playing that day. He definitely would be, Clough informed him, 'But if it makes you play better, have a drink.' If players tried to absent themselves from proceedings – as Archie Gemmill did before the League Cup Final in 1979 – he made their attendance compulsory. Clough had ordered dozens of bottles of champagne, believing that the team were too quiet. For those who preferred it, he bought them pints of bitter. It would be 1am before they made it to bed, after being regaled by Clough and Taylor's tales of their time at Hartlepools. These would have included, among many other memories, the time they had persuaded a local brewery, Cameron's, to pay the wages of one player they wished to sign. Listening that night, Garry Birtles was so drunk that he made it back to his hotel room on his hands and knees.

Sadly, by the early 1990s, his genius was on the wane. He had begun drinking heavily since the mid-1980s and in his last few seasons at the helm vodka had been replaced by Scotch as his preferred tipple. During the final 18 months of his tenure, the booze was evident in his pallor and, unfortunately, in Forest's results. They won just ten matches and conceded 62 goals during his final season.

The media – many of whom were aware of what lay behind it – held back from reporting the full story until those final months of his reign. Some contend that if they had made more of it, Clough could have been helped. The man himself would later realise as much himself. 'On reflection,' he wrote in his second autobiography, 'I'm sure the drink clouded my judgement during that final, fateful season in management.' He believed that had he not been impaired in this way, the club would not have been relegated. 'Drink advanced and contributed to it,' he added.

At the end of the first Premiership season, Forest were down. Clough's behaviour – often questionable – had become ever more erratic. Those final years were increasingly rocky but the signs were there earlier in his career. The earliest flickers of what would follow came shortly after Clough had retired from his playing career in 1964, a decision that was forced upon him through a knee injury at the tail end of 1962. Not only was he no longer able to play the game he loved, he had lost the income that this provided at just the time Clough and his wife needed it most: as his first son was soon to enter the world. After the birth, Clough got drunk, ordering champagne at Wetherall's Club. When he arrived at the hospital, staff were reluctant to let him in to see baby Simon and required him to don a mask to cover his mouth. 'Welcome to fatherhood,' he wrote. Pointing to the injury that ended his playing career, he would reflect: 'I went berserk for a time. I drank heavily. I wasn't very manly.'

There are conflicting accounts of Clough's drinking during this early era: some swore that they had never seen him drunk, others would insist he was near-permanently sozzled. The Clough family's chief complaint about *The Damned United* was that it overplayed the boozy aspects of his time at Leeds. According to Jonathan Wilson's biographical account of the man, Len Ashurst – a player alongside Clough at Sunderland – said that his former team-mate was never the same person after the injury that curtailed his career. 'No one knew how hard it hit me,' Clough wrote. His wife, Barbara, sees his truncated playing career as the reason why he was so hungry for recognition as his management career progressed.

Derby County had been the club where officials had taken the step of locking the drinks cabinet in Clough's office, a man who had been more or less teetotal as a player. Here, Peter Taylor was Clough's accomplice not just in the dugout but in the barroom too, though he sought to minimise both of their proclivity to drink. 'We were both drinking to excess,' he wrote. 'It was a temptation because it was always available. Sometimes I'd take a bottle home. Having said that, Brian's drinking wasn't a problem to me. If I saw him overdoing it, I only had to say "You've had enough," and he'd stop.' Even so, there was a widespread feeling that Clough was unable to operate without champagne in his vicinity and that getting between him and his supply was inadvisable. When he and Taylor were forced out of Derby, he took the players to a country hotel and ordered 30 bottles of champagne.

By Clough's own admission 'booze [was] part of the managerial scene, part and parcel of my business'. Elsewhere, he declared 'drink is readily available. It is always there if you want it. It is provided and it is free ... You have a drink with the chairman ... Because of its availability, if you are not very careful, drink becomes a habit which is extremely difficult to break.' Jimmy Gordon, Clough's first right-hand man, said of his boss: 'He thinks he's indestructible.' He clarified that he did not see it as problematic. 'I know he likes a drink to help with the pressures of the job,' he said, 'but it's never interfered with his work that I know and I've never seen him drunk.'

He hid bottles in his tracksuit pocket and made grand bargains with players where he would promise to give up alcohol as long as the individual concerned at any given instance would stop smoking or some other vice. In the early days, Clough's favoured tipple was brandy or Scotch but he sometimes turned to vodka because he thought – as many drinkers do – that its smell would be harder to detect on his breath. So skilled was he at concealing it from certain figures that even when he had conceded he had a drink problem, they could not believe it.

Clough would drink to ease the pressure on himself, but the drink would instigate its own pressures. Then followed more drinking and more pressure. In 2000 he sat down for an interview with Tyne Tees television, seven years after he had retired. He reflected that alcohol 'encourages you to have a drink because of the strain and pressure you're under. When you finish something and it's over and it's been building up and you run your hands and say, "We haven't done badly today."' He used alcohol to cope with the stresses and alleviate the lows as well as to celebrate – and perhaps heighten – the highs, saying, 'You'd enjoy your success and drown your sorrows.'

When Peter Taylor died in October 1990, many saw this as another pivotal moment in Clough's slow descent. His drinking increased as he tried to deal with the grief of his friend's death. Others say that this is when the problem started altogether. One thing is for sure: it was in that final season that his difficulties with alcohol became plain to see. Clough lacked energy and he was making strange decisions, not least when it came to team selection. His players were vastly undertrained and lacked anywhere near the match fitness required to perform well as their rivals improved.

In those last months of management, Clough only showed up at the training ground on Friday mornings and on Saturday afternoon for match days. 'It is right,' he wrote much later, 'that I should carry the blame.' It was a disastrous season which saw Forest return to where Clough had found them: in the second tier. His past glories could not conceal what was happening now, despite his protestations, 'Booze? I'll give you booze. My decision to retire from the game I've lived in for a lifetime is based simply on the fact that Ol' Big 'Ead has just had enough. That's all.' In January 2003, ten years after leaving the game, Clough had a liver transplant but would sadly die of stomach cancer, aged 69, in September 2004.

'If I had consumed as much alcohol as the lurid tales suggest,' he wrote, 'then I would have been dead years ago.' Clough used his first autobiography to mount a qualified defence of his drinking, though he conceded, 'I do drink too much. In the eyes of a teetotaller, I drink far too much, but then to a non-drinker one half of beer is more than enough.' He added that it was something which 'according to family and friends' should 'preferably be cut[...] out altogether'. Even at this stage, he talked defensively of his drinking, writing in the final chapter: 'I have reached the moment for me to take a grip on the habit, to address it and make sure it never again gets out of hand,' yet still concluding, despite those words, 'I honestly do not see my liking for a drink as a major problem in my life.'

If he was coy in his first autobiography, he had become far more candid by the time his second was published a decade later. Yet even then, he studiously avoided the label 'alcoholic', a term he hated. 'I object to clever buggers who are quick to brand somebody an alcoholic,' he said. Though he believed the work of Alcoholics Anonymous was 'admirable, incredible', he wrote that 'I haven't been in touch because I've never felt the need ...' A reckoning had come when he required a liver transplant in 2002, after which he came to terms with the fact that he could not drink again. 'Drink is not an issue any more ...' he wrote. 'I haven't touched alcohol for well over a year and although I will often be faced with temptation it is simply no longer an option.' Told that he would die if he continued on the same course, he admitted, 'I have to accept that my excessive drinking caused the need for my transplant.'

'I wish I hadn't drunk so much,' wrote this newly reflective Clough. His sons, Nigel and Simon, had mostly cut off contact with him after his retirement from management because of his inability to come to terms with what they saw as his issues around alcohol. His wife, Barbara, had been upset by it too. 'I don't,' Clough said, 'know what normal is in a drinking sense.'

9.

THE WOOD FROM THE TREES

ROGER Milford was the man who oversaw the 1991 FA Cup Final between Tottenham Hotspur and Nottingham Forest. He was the one who tried to talk Paul Gascoigne down after he had made a high challenge on Garry Parker, catching him in the chest. Milford's mediation failed when, shortly afterwards, Gascoigne chopped down Gary Charles as he marauded into the Spurs box. Brian Clough called it 'the day I witnessed the worst refereeing decision in my 40-odd years in football'. His annoyance seemed to stem from Gascoigne's recklessness, during which he had incurred the same injury which had ended Clough's own time as a player by tearing the cruciate ligament. Though he was far from alone in this, he did not like seeing injured players, reminders of how he was forced to quit the game at 29.

He was furious that Gascoigne had remained on the field long enough to injure himself after a series of rash challenges. The north Londoners got away with conceding a free kick but would ultimately pay when Stuart Pearce belted it into their net. Gascoigne would pay too. His challenge on Charles led to the cruciate ligament injury to his right knee which nearly scuppered his move to Lazio. When he eventually arrived at the Stadio Olimpico, fans displayed a banner reading 'Gazza's Boys Are Here ... Shag Women, Drink Beer'.

Terry Venables was in charge of Tottenham that day. He and Clough held hands as they emerged onto the Wembley turf, amid suspicions that Clough was several sheets to the wind. Clough later described it as 'a little gesture between rival managers on the one day of the season that is more special than the rest'. Instead, it became a bitter day. He had failed to win the FA Cup once again and would never have the pleasure of holding it aloft. Some think he would have retired there and then – a happy man – had Forest won, but it was not to be. Gascoigne had been on the verge of signing for Lazio and his enthusiasm about bidding farewell to England with a winner's medal and a memorable performance had got the better of him.

❧

'I still don't know why I didn't jump it,' Gary Charles, known as 'gazelle' by Clough, told the *Birmingham Mail* of Gascoigne's challenge. Charles now has a clinic, GCSportsCare, which assists sportspeople and professionals dealing with issues around addiction and unmanageability. 'If I could help one person, it will all be worthwhile – 100 per cent,' he said at its launch. Charles, who did Clough's gardening for £20 as a young apprentice, is sober 13 years as of 2019.

It had been a winding road to get there. When chatting to a fellow inmate during his incarceration in HMP Ashwell, his inquisitor asked him what he did when he made a mistake on the pitch. Charles replied that he tried to learn from it to avoid repeating the same thing again. 'He just looked at me and said, "Why don't you apply that attitude to your drinking then?" Those words stuck in my head.'

Because of his addiction, the player reckoned that he only got 'about 50 per cent' of what he could have out of football, and when he left the game things unravelled quickly. There were prison sentences – one for drink-driving, another for assault on a bouncer – and a third suspended for another assault. When he was sentenced in 2006, the judge remarked that 'everyone needs a rest from Gary Charles'. There had been other incidents, albeit non-custodial, in 1993 and 1998.

The signs had been there while he was still playing. Perhaps because as a player his drinking took the form of binges, his managers – including Harry Redknapp and, of course, Clough – never fully got wind of the road he was heading down. 'Footballers can have the same problems as a postman or plumber,' he explained in a newspaper interview. 'Millions watch them on a Saturday but some suffer in silence. It's hard for them to own up. Will it be detrimental to their next contract? Will they be replaced?'

Like Clough, Charles was capped twice by England. The story of Charles's call-up, however, is one tainted by tragedy. His team-mates had informed him that he had been included in the national squad, but he could not believe it and headed out to get a newspaper from the shop to see it for himself. The print confirmed it, but on his way home a cyclist overtook him on the wrong side and Charles collided with him as he turned in his car. The verdict, of accidental death, was devastating and something the player kept to himself for a long time. He played for Forest on the night of the accident, his team-mates oblivious to those events.

That incident would not have helped matters, but Charles had been using alcohol to mask his shyness since his teenage years. He had a foray into Alcoholics Anonymous in his 20s, but it did not stick back then. Now, he's a regular. 'I am relieved to know that I was an alcoholic,' he said to one newspaper, 'because I know what I need to do to live the happy life I have today. I want to help people understand they can get their lives back.' The mid-1990s had been particularly challenging after a horrifying ankle injury while at Villa put him out of football for two years. Such was the severity of the injury that Dwight Yorke was crying on the pitch when his foot dislocated from the ankle.

At Forest, Charles had often shared a room in digs with Roy Keane and it was the Cork man who would offer to come to his aid when he was nearing the end of his term in prison. Keane wrote to him offering a job at Sunderland – he was managing at the Stadium of Light at the time – and a place to stay in the family home. It's a side of Keane that is not often seen and something that he is reticent to see mentioned too often. His kindness to Charles would mean that the former defender would have a place to stay and adjust to a new life. Through running training drills, Charles was given the opportunity to lead, giving him a taste of the future career he would dip his toe in to. He already had some experience in taking responsibility for a team, having taken charge of the prison football side when they had a match against the guards.

Having retired in 2002, four years later Charles was sober and building a new life. Since then there have been spells in the management structures of Lincoln City and Nuneaton Town, as well as some scouting work. With an Open University qualification in substance abuse under his belt, he sees a place for his own business today in a climate where footballers are averse to confiding in anyone around their employer. 'Would I have gone to one of my coaches and admitted my alcohol problems? No. Did I know I had them at that time? Maybe not,' he explained to the *Daily Mail*. 'It's hard to think you may have serious issues at 19. It's still seen as a weakness now, in life and in sport.'

This is understandable on several levels: can you imagine going to your boss and telling him you cannot stop drinking in the morning? 'I still don't believe many footballers would go in-house with a problem,' he continued. 'You may rather come to my team of counsellors, wouldn't you, in the hope that nobody at work would find out? So, from that point of view, things haven't changed much from my day … they push people to us and it works.'

❧

That 'us' is GCSportsCare, which Charles runs alongside Lorna McClelland, who previously worked as a player liaison officer at Aston Villa. Her role at the Birmingham

The Freemasons' Tavern in Covent Garden, London. The Football Association was founded here in October 1863.

John Houlding dressed in his mayoral regalia. He founded Liverpool FC in 1892.

Hughie Gallacher, c. 1935. He was capped by Scotland 20 times.

George Best arrives in London after Manchester United's European Cup victory over Benfica in Lisbon in 1966.

Best sips from a pint in a Belfast pub, c. 1970.

Jimmy Greaves makes his debut for West Ham in March 1970.

Brian Clough with a Manager of the Month award in 1979.

Best is arrested on drink-driving charges in late 1984.

Alex Ferguson with Paul McGrath and Bryan Robson in February 1987.

Steve Morrow, Ian Wright, Tony Adams and Ray Parlour with the FA Cup in January 1993.

Paul Merson confesses to his addictions in December 1994.

Arsene Wenger arrives at Arsenal in November 1996.

Arsene Wenger and Tony Adams present the FA Cup and Premiership trophy in Islington.

'Dry Your Eyes, Mate' – Paul Merson during a 2-2 draw with Derby County in December 1996.

Paul Gascoigne celebrates in the 'Dentist's Chair' after scoring the second goal in England's 2-0 victory over Scotland at Euro 96.

Paul Merson and Paul Gascoigne celebrate Middlesbrough's promotion to the Premier League in May 1998.

club was an interesting one and one that had not existed before – certainly not with the definitions it has today – when she arrived at Villa Park in 2002. Was it the dawning of a new footballing era which created a need for someone like her? 'Yes,' she told me. 'I contacted Graham Taylor, who was the manager at the time, to suggest that the club look at providing both language support for foreign players, and practical support to players and families – with a counselling service as part of an umbrella approach. He asked me to come and meet him, and we discussed the provision of such a service as he had been considering the need for something like this.'

She was given an office and a set of keys and told to work out what her job should entail. 'He eventually created a post,' she said, and Lorna went on to pioneer a new approach to player welfare which has since been adopted by every other football club as well as within other sporting institutions. 'I saw a change in the way that club staff worked together, and that clubs offered a more holistic approach to the care of a player. The doctor and physios would regularly communicate with the player liaison, so that a player's care was the best that it could possibly be.'

That close relationship with the medical department is never more crucial than in the case of players sidelined through long-term injury. 'Players need not only practical but emotional support when a long-term injury arises,' Lorna explained, 'because often the player will have no idea of the potential implications on his relationships and family life.' Lorna is a great advocate of 'family support' in player care, but sees close relationships within the team as vital: 'If a player is "off the scene" for a while, players often regroup, sharing new jokes, experiences and stories. The injured player is marginalised, and will often turn to drugs, alcohol or gambling for solace, stimulation or excitement because they offer the sense of belonging that he might miss.'

Famously, Bill Shankly would not talk to an injured player, seeing them as – at best – distractions from the objective of winning football matches and league titles. Several decades later, when his fellow Scotsman George Graham became Tottenham manager, there was a policy of keeping injured players back until Graham knew the traffic would be at its worst during rush hour on the M25. 'When I arrived,' he told one interviewer, 'I changed the treatment hours – the last session now finishes at 4pm. That's just about when the M25 becomes absolutely hellish. It's surprising how many people now manage to get out of the treatment room well ahead of rush hour.'

During her 15 years at Bodymoor Heath, Lorna's was a hands-on role: 'I was at the training ground every day, and players – particularly foreign players – found it extremely helpful that I was there in case they needed to speak with the doctor, physio, coaches or even the manager, and vice versa. Good communication is vital to the smooth running of a club. We also had a counselling service that was available to all players, and the fact that I was there daily meant that often issues could be resolved quickly, or certainly that they could be addressed by someone they could trust.'

Graham Taylor left Aston Villa a year after Lorna's appointment and she operated under a further seven managers following his departure. 'Everyone with whom I worked,' said Lorna, 'was more than aware of the majority of the things taking place in their players' lives and – at times – certain comments from team-mates or certain behaviours on the part of the player made potential problems all too obvious.' Managers, of course, are not immune from addictions and Lorna recalled one former manager with whom she worked 'who is still greatly revered for his harsh treatment of players years ago, and his proffering of a drink to players before the game!'

A manager's previous experience as a player will often shape his modus operandi when dealing with players who are coping with addictions. Lorna explained, 'They may be supportive of efforts to deal with the issues facing a player, but they may equally be very reticent to do so – "oh, he's just being one of the lads". It is obviously very important for a player to feel that he "belongs" and this can lead them to make some very poor choices.'

Though the game has clearly progressed in the last 25 years, there are still aspects which Lorna sees as being problematic. 'There is even more pressure on younger players to succeed, and their families often inadvertently increase this pressure.' Then there's the dressing room. 'The "elephant in the room" is, of course, bullying,' Lorna said. 'This is endemic in football, and is often accepted as being the norm. It has always been present, and there are still coaches in clubs who regard themselves as "old school", and continue to bully people at all levels, but in particular, academy players.'

'It's an extremely worrying and common problem,' Lorna told me. 'Victims are generally frightened about speaking up or of seeking support within the club structure. Plainly, this is because it could adversely affect their career, or even snuff it out before it has even started. This is a fear that is not without foundation.' Continuing, she explained: 'People outside football may not realise that even coaches and managers may experience bullying. Clubs are far more open these days about the problem, and many do their best to tackle it. However, there are still some clubs in which players are not adequately supported in this matter, and where a player will suddenly cease to be given a place in the team, as he has become a "trouble maker".' Lorna believes there is still a lot to be done in order to eradicate bullying.

'The fact that one person was responsible,' she said, 'for the overall welfare off the pitch meant that any changes in a player's behaviour could be quickly picked up and dealt with at the outset.' With a trend towards outsourcing the player liaison responsibilities, Lorna sees the human aspects of players' lives being compartmentalised, with no single individual ultimately looking out for their welfare. 'Now they often don't feel that they have someone to confide in, should they need some discreet help.' That trusted individual is disappearing at larger clubs, to be replaced by separate consultants for language provision, counselling, accommodation and cars. 'As football increasingly becomes a sophisticated business,' Lorna said, 'the human aspect of the game should be addressed more deeply; clubs shouldn't lose sight of the individuals within it, and how they are cared for.'

This is where she sees the value in her work with Charles at GCSportsCare, which provides 'a confidential support system for sportspeople who are experiencing difficulties'. With Charles's own journey through addiction, and Lorna's years of experience at Villa, they work with players to tackle their issues while becoming independent and – of course – limiting any disruption to their sporting life and training schedule. Where alcohol is involved, as it often is, she believes it is 'vital to identify problems early on, and to be able to "nip them in the bud"'. Warning signs might be tiredness in training, sleeping difficulties or, for some, aggression in social situations inside or outside the club.

'Depression and anxiety are also common pointers,' Lorna went on to explain. A bad diet outside the training ground as well as poor grooming and personal hygiene are sometimes tell-tale indicators of inner turmoil. 'Players could be experiencing homesickness or a lack of confidence, and alcohol could soothe these issues temporarily. Clubs tend to become aware of such problems very quickly, as these changes are seen by team-mates and support staff. Quite often, problems are noted following a game, or when the team travels away.' At this point, the player liaison is made aware that there is a situation to be dealt with. 'A team-mate would sometimes mention it to me in confidence,' Lorna said. 'It was then up to me to find a way of broaching the subject with the player.' At other times, it might be a player's wife or partner who approached Lorna, when his plight was not evident to his team-mates.

'One of the most difficult things is how to manage the problem without breaking confidentiality, if other members of staff needed to be made aware,' Lorna said, shedding light on the specifics of this process. She would speak to the player about how he wanted her to proceed, but she would never break his confidence: 'If you lose the trust of a player, you can never regain it, and deservedly so.' Lorna would work on a strategy which she would suggest to the manager – usually fitting into the club's schedules – to seek his approval on a plan of action.

'I would sometimes be the person who was initially approached about a drink problem, in particular. Generally, we would seek an appropriate next step, which was either the club doctor or a specialist-led support group, where appropriate. At this stage, the manager would have to be informed, with the knowledge of the player, and I would often suggest a meeting together with him – that first stage can be pretty frightening for a player, particularly a young one,' Lorna said. When a spell in residential treatment was required, there would be an attempt to minimise time away from training and matches by, if possible, coinciding their stay with an international break.

What is clear is that respect was paid to the nuances and requirements of a given individual. 'Each case was a learning situation,' she said, 'as every player is, of course, different. They have different needs and will cope with addiction in different ways, so every individual situation needs to be handled with great care and the personality involved needs to be carefully considered.'

Her role, Lorna said as we concluded our exchange, was to provide an 'umbrella' of support 'similar to that of a parent'. Several members of staff were involved in the ongoing process of treating and monitoring the player until they were satisfied that he was improving. In cases where players might be forming bad habits around substances, there were regular informal seminars at which former sportspeople came to speak about their problems with addiction. 'These sessions were frank and sometimes hard-hitting in their honesty, and struck a chord with more than one player,' she said. 'But they had the chance to contact the speakers for private conversations, if they needed them.' These conversations, as we will discover in the next chapter, are often life-changing moments.

10.

DOWN THE WINDING ROAD

'No other habit or culturally determined
behaviour pattern creates more medical
problems than does alcohol abuse' –
George Vaillant

'I am a recovering alcoholic, never a
recovered alcoholic' – Tony Adams

I N 1882 a Connecticut doctor, J.E. Todd, published a pamphlet which contained the following passage: 'Every human is worth saving; but what I mean is, that if a choice is to be made, drunkards are about the last class to be taken hold of.' There was a sense that alcoholics were so baffling that, as a group, they ought to be regarded as irredeemable. Sure, you might be able to save some of them but so many of them did not seem to *want* to be saved, so there was no point in trying too hard.

One hundred years earlier, Benjamin Rush had pioneered ideas around the disease model of alcoholism, having been a distinguished colonial-era doctor and physician and a signatory of the Declaration of Independence. His book, *Medical Inquiries and Observations upon the Diseases of the Mind*, was published in 1784 and took the form of a treatise on alcoholism as a condition that required treatment as opposed to incarceration or punishment. Within its pages, he created the concept of 'sober houses', special hospitals which would be an early incarnation of the treatment centre.

When it came to matters of treatment and punishment, the late 19th century saw a shift in the British government's view of alcoholism – the state of 'habitual drunkenness' – from that of a pure vice to conceding that there could be some form of disease being responsible. A parliamentary act dealing with these matters was passed in 1879 which allowed retreats for 'compulsive drunkards' to be created. Yet entrance to such facilities was voluntary and the costs were borne by the patient, although inmates – which is what they were, once they had offered themselves up to the administrators – were not allowed to leave until they had completed their treatment.

The same act also clarified the term 'habitual drunkard' itself, defining it as referring to 'a person who by means of habitual intemperate drinking of intoxicating liquor is dangerous to himself ... or others ... or incapable of managing himself or herself, and his or her affairs.' Such a person would have to be confined to the aforementioned retreat and it was a magistrate – rather than a doctor – who would sign off on their fate, a reflection of the continuing ambiguity over how the condition was regarded by those in power. Unsurprisingly, this new system was wildly unsuccessful: you had to be rich to commit to it since you were paying the costs yourself, willing to put yourself before the court and then, finally, consent to being locked away for up to a year. Five years after the act had passed, only six such facilities existed, treating a grand total of 45 patients.

By 1898 another act had been passed by parliament, this time stipulating that patients could be forcibly sent away to dry out. This created two levels of facility: one type of locally managed institution and another level of state-managed reformatories. The latter were managed by the Home Secretary and designated for the worst offenders to be served as part of their prison sentence. Alternatively, minor repeat offenders could be directed to one closer to home with a lighter touch, although it could be three years before they were allowed their freedom.

Some 100 years later, Tony Adams had been sober for a couple of years and began to feel that players he had spoken to in a similar position to his own at the end of Euro 96 needed to get playing as quickly as possible. Adams had identified a need for something specific to the needs of sportsmen. The Priory did great work as specialists in addiction, but they were not geared to the particular requirements of the sportsman, who needed to remain remarkably fit in order to carry out his job. Now a few years without a drink and with a reasonable bank balance, Adams believed he could help people like himself. Sporting Chance was born, owing its name to Mandy Jacobs, wife of Arsenal's player-liaison, Steve. It soon listed Elton John as a patron.

The PFA's Gordon Taylor had been burned – financially and otherwise – by other treatment centres he had sent his members to for their addictions. This gave him a greater willingness to back Sporting Chance, using union funds to – as Adams put it – 'help us help his members'. Though happy with this backing, it was important to Adams and his advisors that the charity did not become the treatment wing of one particular club or organisation. Fiercely guarding its independence, Sporting Chance was careful to ensure that the help it gave to players was not seen as an enforced punishment meted through their club. When Taylor revealed to him which players were currently struggling and might benefit from the organisation's help, Adams could have predicted most of them. As the adage goes, 'it takes one to know one'.

In its earliest incarnation, Sporting Chance operated on a fairly ad hoc basis, mainly dealing with players on a one-to-one basis in temporary settings where players' privacy was hard to guarantee. It was when Stephen Purdew offered the use of two cottages at the Champney's spa resort in Hampshire – away from prying eyes – that the charity was finally able to begin offering a dedicated service to players.

Among their number since then is Drewe Broughton. He had 22 clubs over his 17-year professional career which began in what was then Division One in 1996 with Norwich City. By the time it drew to a close in 2012, with Darlington in the Conference National, Broughton was at an emotional rock bottom. His problem was not drink, nor drugs, or even alcohol. Rather it was what he describes in his autobiography as 'emotional damage and traumas that acted out as addictive tendencies'. There may have been occasions when too many beers were taken, but primarily he would use women for sex and affection before discarding them. Eventually, he was fed up of his own behaviour and turned to the PFA for help. Clarke Carlisle, chairman of the players' association, phoned the Sporting Chance clinic and arranged for Broughton to go to Hampshire for an assessment.

In *And Then What …?* Broughton wrote of his arrival, which involved driving down a long and winding road through a dense wood, describing the strategically placed speed bumps along the way to the cottages as giving him a sense of peace. He had been given instructions: 'Go past the big house. The road bends to the left and you will see a small track, go down here and about 400 metres on the left you'll see a gate and a cottage. Pull into the drive and knock on the door.' This he did and, when he reached his destination, he was greeted by a man named James.

It was the start of a 30-day stay, commencing with a two-hour interview in a quiet room overlooking the woods at Forest Mere, sat in an armchair surrounded by soft furnishings. The purpose was to draw him out of himself, to find out who he was and why he was there. He had been told by a friend, 'Don't let them put the God shit on you,' but he found mentions of the Divine extremely rare and framed in deliberately vague terms: 'a God of his own understanding'.

His visit, whether he knew it or not, was about building a new foundation. It helped that his days had a structure and daily discipline that had been lacking for some time. He would get up at 7.30am and meet with the two other sportsmen undergoing this process in the small lounge downstairs. After breakfast he would go for a run in the 'vast and beautiful' woodland at the Champney's resort. This was supplemented by use of the swimming pool and gym at the facility, fitting in around his daily one-to-one therapy sessions which took their shape from AA's 12-step model. It was a set of guidelines which Broughton feels ought to be integrated into the training that prospective coaches receive when getting their FA badges.

When another footballer, Christian Roberts, had visited for a spell in 2006, he was surprised. The striker, who had spells with Cardiff City, Bristol City and Swindon Town, had been expecting something a bit glitzier: the celebrity rehabs you see on American television shows. Not this quiet, isolated location in the middle of the Hampshire countryside. It wasn't until November 2005 that he had come to the realisation that there was something wrong with his drinking and that he would have to do something about it. After seeing a picture of Calum Best in a newspaper next to the player's declining father, Roberts went to see his manager, Iffy Onuora, who mentioned that he had noticed his player had been drinking a lot. It was the first time anyone had addressed this with Roberts, however lightly, in a professional capacity. Onoura told him he could have the next week off 'to take a look at himself', and Roberts left the manager's office with a choice to make. He came to a decision quickly, returning to tell his boss, 'Iffy, I need help.'

Onuora had been testing him, making sure that he wanted to be helped. He immediately got on the phone to Peter Kay from Sporting Chance. When Onuora put Roberts on the line, Kay told the footballer: 'I've been waiting all year for you to call.' Arriving after Christmas, Roberts headed for the smallest of the rooms available to him. 'I wasn't there for luxury, I was there to punish myself.'

Noel Whelan, the former Leeds United youngster whose football career was now on an interminable slide, was there too and each of them had a weigh-in at the beginning of their treatment programme. Roberts had imagined that he might be a little overweight due to all the alcohol he had been throwing down his neck, but when the scales reported a body fat rating of 21 per cent, he was horrified. A professional footballer should find himself between six and ten per cent.

❧❧

The stories of these players piqued my interest and I wanted to better understand the inner workings of Sporting Chance. Following several emails, in late 2018 I made a three-legged train journey to the Hampshire–Sussex border and, amid the tinkling of cutlery on china in the busy tea room at the Champney's resort, I spoke to Colin Bland.

'Quite often,' the Sporting Chance CEO told me, 'what makes people great at sport is the fact that they don't feel so great about themselves. They will practice and practice to prove that they are good enough. If we're looking at assessing someone, we will normally look at their genetics: is there any addiction in the family history? We'll normally look at their upbringing and we'll normally look at their current situation.'

Parental influences are important in another context; when the mother or father themselves are addicts and – via nature or nurture – transmit this to the child. 'If one parent has an addictive disorder,' Colin said, 'there's a 25 per cent increased chance [that their child will be an addict], if both parents it's 50 per cent, so it is a factor as it would be in normal life, but it's a factor that's then compounded by an environment that's terribly pressured.'

Writing in the 1970s, the French neurophysiologist Henri Begleiter saw genes as being responsible for between 40 and 60 per cent of the risk factor of being an alcoholic. Begleiter's research was responsible for changing the way many viewed alcoholism and its causes. He suggested that, as young children, potential 'alcoholics' had a pre-existing hyper-excitability before they were even exposed to a drop of alcohol or any other substance. The 'madness' is already there and alcohol is used to feed it, rather than the drink being the root cause of the insanity itself.

'We'll normally look at what they believe about themselves,' Colin continued, 'and what they believe about the world. When we're assessing people, they tell us they strive to train and be good enough and practice and practice and practice, which makes them a good player, sometimes based on the fact that they don't feel good enough. So I think there is a propensity for, actually, what breeds success is the fear of failure.' Evidence suggests that alcoholism among professional athletes could be up to double that of the general population, linked to their high-risk, high-reward lifestyle.

The expectation to perform at the top of their game, sometimes beyond their innate ability, can place them under pressures which some will seek to alleviate through patterns of behaviour which can become addictive. Colin had a theory, 'that even if we worked with plumbers and not sportspeople, for every hundred plumbers that we came across there would be a percentage that were going to be addicts or alcoholics. Is that slightly higher in sport? I think it is.

'There's research that says that professional sportspeople are three times more likely to have a gambling problem. Gambling does seem to be the drug of choice in football at the moment. Football's changed so much that people can't drink the way that they used to drink maybe ten years ago, 15 years ago, 20 years ago. So that is something about the structure of sport, the pressure of sport, the culture that actually does breed or give that greenhouse to an addictive disorder.'

The athlete lives with a constant element of doubt, which – to a greater or lesser extent – we all do. Yet for a sportsman even success cannot quell the whispers because, invariably, there are still bigger victories to be had. Only a few can be champions and, anyway, what is a single league title? A fluke, that's what. If I work for the second-biggest company in my sector, I'm probably fairly happy with that. If I finish second in the Premier League, I'm a bottler and a failure.

Footballing autobiographies, abundant as they are, will talk of concepts like willpower and grit, and these are undoubted factors in success, but it is so often their flaws – genetic or otherwise – that helped their authors get where they are. Sometimes, a troubled childhood will imbue them with what the authors Paul Gogarty and Ian Williamson term 'psychological hypervigilance'. Their ability to vocalise or even process their reaction to circumstances are beyond the control of the psychologically troubled sportsman. The world, to them, is a threatening place, so they look for something that they *can* affect some control over.

For somebody like Paul Gascoigne, this meant overdeveloped physical skills honed through relentless, repeated practice. 'I didn't have twitches or worry when I was playing football,' he said. He was safe while he was on the pitch with its clearly defined rules and roles to play, but off it he didn't know what to do other than drink or act out in other harmful ways.

It may be that this *-ism* personality type is one well suited to reaching the heights of professional sport. Single-minded determination, open to high risks in order to achieve high rewards, obsessive about fulfilling potential and being the best they can be. That's great, but with it comes the compulsiveness of the alcoholic too. To some, that individual might appear like a devious, difficult character. Those last aspects cannot be overstated. Players are often held up as either clowns, evil or both when their antics carry them from the back to the front pages. The reality is far more complicated. They are flawed, sometimes broken men who are terrified of themselves and the trail of wreckage and dramatic headlines they leave in their wake, sometimes unable to stop doing the thing that has propelled them there. As Colin put it during our discussion, 'You get some players who get labelled as "problems". Are they a problem or do they *have* a problem? That's a different conversation.'

The alcohol fuels the madness and, lacking what Gogarty and Williamson call 'internal authority', somebody like Gascoigne will oscillate between feelings of extreme elation and desolation. To an onlooking public, the pranks and practical jokes are amusing, 'daft as a brush' as Bobby Robson put it. But they mask an inadequacy, a fear. The game itself is – either through negligence or lack of understanding – ill-equipped to deal with these outsized personalities. Gascoigne's tears at Italia 90 preceded the onset of his most worrying drinking. He could – and should – have been helped much earlier and were he a snooker player, Gogarty and Williamson argue, most likely would have been. Managers, though, are employed to create winning teams ahead of nurturing balanced individuals.

❧❧

In 2019 Sporting Chance has the contract for delivering education around alcohol addiction to academies, providing a stripped-back version to the under-16 age groups and a no-holds barred analysis to the under-18s. Modern clubs, especially at elite academy level, are looking to generate well-rounded people – not simply footballers – given the fact that 99 per cent of those who go through the academy system will not be playing professional football a few years later. There is now a greater acceptance of the fact that these clubs have a responsibility both to the individuals and the world at large to avoid chewing them up and spitting them out as damaged goods at 18 or 21.

Those elite academies will put the kids in their care into private, fee-paying schools at age seven in which they will be taught normally three days of the week and dedicate themselves solely to football during the other two. For Manchester City, that is £8,000 per year St Bedes. Only really mixing with other footballers, they are primed in an atmosphere where they become accustomed to a certain lifestyle – things provided and done for them – which, for most of them, will come crashing down at the stroke of an administrative pen while they are still learning to shave. Then begins the process of picking up the pieces, coming to terms with the broken dreams. For some, that's a life-shattering process, and a few of those – with no discernible skills other than kicking a ball – will throw themselves into the bottle.

'The thing to remember about football,' says Colin, 'is that it's so deep and multi-layered, we deal with everyone from the elite Premier League clubs down to people who have just been demoted to the Conference and, going down to quite a deep level, a lot of those clubs run academies or have programmes where they're trying to bring young players through.

'At the elite level, Premier League, Championship and even just below that the academies are really quite structured and there's an awful lot of input that goes into those academies that is about trying to make young *children* football players but at the same time give them a life experience and become rounded. So, we do a lot of education and life-skills training. The academies have a whole lifestyle segment that they work through in their education.' In the clinic's formative years, Sir Alex Ferguson granted them permission to hold a seminar at Carrington, imposing a three-line whip to ensure that not just youth-teamers but the entire first-team squad were in attendance.

'You can have all the money in the world,' Colin said, picking up the thread, 'but at some football clubs *football* is too important and people become less important, so actually it is about finding a balance in an age where children can join a Premier League academy from age eight. So all of a sudden you've got children thinking that they're going to be a professional footballer, they're children and it has to be respected that they are children – and people – first, and football players second.'

There is a concern that teenagers getting academy scholarships that require them to up sticks, possibly hundreds of miles away from their families for long periods of time could be storing up problems in these players' lives. It is a fear which Colin shares: 'The thing to remember is that only one per cent of them are going to end up being elite football players, so you've got a big problem, which is why football is trying to spend so much time at the moment trying to focus on the whole individual, trying to get these children to really appreciate the opportunity they've got as a person rather than being so invested. But one of the problems is not so much that the children get invested that they are going to be a football player. It's that the whole family does, the idea that "he's gonna be the next big thing". It puts an awful lot of pressure on a child when their family are so invested in their success. I was listening to someone talk earlier about a young player of 12 who was going to be the next best thing, he was going to be great, all this pressure on him, and he ended up not wanting to play anymore. I think there is something "in the post" but I think football is trying to do something about that.'

'The worry is with the young players,' Colin said as we shared some tea, 'is that they are away from home. You've got 14-, 16-year-olds who could be 300 miles away from home. It used to be that you had to live two hours from the club whose academy you were signed to and now that's changed and you can be anywhere in the country. So now, Chelsea could sign an eight-year-old from Newcastle. That's a massive change in the rules that has meant there's a lot of children away from home.'

When one of the fortunate few players leaves the academy and enters the first-team squad, the contrast with what had gone before is stark. Now they are at the mercy of the manager and his assistants, and where the various leagues have a legal obligation to academy scholars, the realms of adult football are dictated by the whims of one or two men who control whether the players in his charge will be given time to address the issues they are facing up to. Many clubs have frameworks in place for such eventualities and deal with these matters well, though that is not the case across the board. Broadly speaking, though, there is an emphasis on holism that had been conspicuously absent in previous decades and Sporting Chance has adapted its own offering in order to cater to players dealing with predicaments beyond addictive disorders.

Only around a third of the clients the clinic sees through its doors these days are dealing specifically with alcohol addiction. The simple fact is it would be nearly impossible to play at the top level while maintaining a heavy drinking habit in 2019. On top of this, many of the sportspeople with addictive personalities who present themselves to Sporting Chance are dealing with a gambling problem or an addiction to a prescribed drug, compulsions which will evade detection by doping testers or even beady-eyed club officials. Skirting round these issues in their personal lives often stores up problems until a player reaches their sporting retirement age. Typically, this will be between the ages of 32 and 35, when they are free to cut loose and indulge these behaviours without fear of damaging their professional career. Many will have suppressed the alcohol-related aspect of their addiction for 15 or 20 years, perhaps binging for a few weeks post-season in the Mediterranean. Once retired, they have the time and resources to do as they please.

'In the current playing population,' Colin spelled out for me, 'alcohol use tends to be binge drinking at times where they get an opportunity to do so, that's the most common pattern of drinking that we see in football players.' Once retired, there's less structure from the game in the absence of any obligation to a club to be physically fit. If there were already signs of an alcohol problem, it is now given space to become a lot more chaotic. While gambling tends to be the most common addiction among active players today, Colin made clear that they 'see a lot more alcohol abuse' among those who have recently hung up their boots.

Typically, then, the active footballers that Sporting Chance has seen in the last decade or so are 'bout' drinkers who will confine the heaviest of their consumption to the close season. Even below the Premier League, the standard of fitness required would not allow for several nights out a week. More often than not, these are players from the Championship or below who have reached a point where they must confront their addiction. A number of them will then have to deal with the reality that they could have played at a higher level had they not drunk away some of their best years. 'I don't know if that is because they don't have the fitness [at a lower level],' Colin theorised, 'so that alcohol is still acceptable or if maybe actually those guys might be playing at a higher level if they didn't have an alcohol problem and they gravitated towards a lower level. It's hard to say, of course everyone thinks they should be playing at a better level, I think that's natural.'

Factor in frequent travel to away games and a fairly transient, rootless lifestyle that a transfer every couple of seasons can bring and you can see how a player could start drinking as a way to cope. Reaching the peak of their profession at a young age, often these players have underdeveloped social skills, masking that through drinking to increasing excess. On a day-to-day basis that can be something which goes undetected for longer than it might in the man on the street, not least because of how fit footballers have to be and how minimal their physical symptoms are by comparison.

Clarke Carlisle spent time at Sporting Chance in 2003. In September of that year he had boarded Queens Park Rangers' team coach for a fixture against Colchester. As he did, he was confronted by his manager Ian Holloway, who could smell alcohol on him as soon as he got on. Holloway grabbed him, asking, 'What the hell are you playing at?' Carlisle tried to brush it off with a joke, telling Holloway he was 'trying to get some sleep'. The player was thrown off the bus and told he was training with the youth team for the next two days. This he did. Well, for one day at least. The next morning he headed to a Yates's bar at 9am and began drinking. By that afternoon, he was in another bar watching *Soccer Saturday*. It was then he had a moment of realisation: he was looking out for the result of the team he was actually being paid to play for. It was a rock bottom.

He walked out of the bar and phoned Holloway as he walked home. In the coming days his boss had him round for a meal with his family and they talked through the situation, which provoked tears from Carlisle. They were partly out of relief at finally coming to terms with what had been going on for the previous few years. Holloway was supportive. He told Carlisle that he could not sort this out for his player, but he knew some people who could help. That's how Carlisle ended up being dispatched to Sporting Chance.

Holloway's plan, had the phone call not come, had been to sack his midfielder by terminating his contract. Instead, the PFA financed Carlisle's treatment and he spent a month under the Sporting Chance regime in Hampshire. His only communication with the outside world while he was in the isolation of Forest Mere was via the medium of pen and paper. His enrolment at the Sporting Chance clinic had come just in time. 'By then I was ready,' he wrote. 'I'd had enough of what I was doing. I was open to learn. I said, "This is me, I think I'm a bit fucked. Strip me down and show me what to do." It was life-changing, because I wanted it to be. I felt fake, I never felt like I was me with anyone. Also, I loved my career and I loved my family and I knew I was going to lose it all if I didn't change my ways.'

There were some guidelines that Sporting Chance had suggested around relationships. More specifically, he had been advised that it might be wise to stay single for a little while. Because he had met someone just before he went in, he was unable to comply: 'I wrote to her a couple of times when I was in there. When I came out, I was supposed to stay single for a year but that didn't happen!' This is an informal suggestion common among 12-step fellowships. Nobody is going to throw you out for disobeying it and the stability of a solid relationship could be a positive but it could equally be a distraction in the wrong circumstances.

Carlisle was just shy of his 24th birthday when he entered the clinic. I asked Colin about the ages of the players coming through their doors. 'It's been really interesting,' he said, 'because it used to be a little bit older, but the current players [that they see] are quite young now; we've got a young guy in treatment at the moment who's 22, in the last treatment episode a guy who was 24, so early to mid-20s is not uncommon.' Is that because of an increased awareness of addiction? 'I think the ones that we'll see, and this is generally as well, people are asking for help earlier and I think in wider society there's been an awful lot of work around mental health. You and me wouldn't be having this conversation ten years ago and I think more people talk about it, pathways are there so people are using them.'

Jeff Whitley, once of Manchester City and Sunderland, is another Sporting Chance graduate. Sober ten years, he continues the practice of going to AA meetings. To neglect the thing that got him to the stable place he now finds himself would have been unthinkable. 'I'm not brave enough to say I'm never ever going to drink,' he told *The Independent* a few years ago. 'It's just a day at a time. I used to think I'm never going to drink again. For me, I've recovered, not from the illness, I've recovered from the mental obsession.' In 2015 he told another newspaper that he believed clubs 'hush up' certain aspects of the daily life of a footballer, not properly educating the young men they are responsible for in how to be a well-rounded individual.

The game, he said, should be doing more for ex-footballers too. His own career ended before he was 30, something which he attributes to his drinking. Entering Sporting Chance in 2007, he has since had a spell in an educational role at the charity, passing on what he learned. He now works in a similar role for the PFA as a qualified counsellor. As well as the one-to-ones, Whitley delivers educational talks to young recruits, particularly on gambling, which he says has 'soared'. 'I let them know they can get counselling if they need it. Because they're so young they might not be at the severity, say, I was.'

The culture of the game has changed. A hard-drinking player in 2019 would be seen as letting his team-mates – and everything they had all worked for – down and he would be told as much. The stakes are so much higher; where once it was just about winning, now the reputational fates of entire nation states rest on their stars performing up to and beyond the required standard. Footballers, being athletes, may be able to mask the physical effects that alcohol is having on their bodies and the ravages to their nervous system because they are so fit. On the other hand, though, the fact that they are performing alongside other people who are so phenomenally fine-tuned mean that on the pitch their being even just several per cent below their best – in a game of extremely fine margins – would be instantly obvious.

❧

There is both an art and a science to the clinic's treatment methods. After the cessation of a prolonged bout of drinking – days, weeks or months – withdrawal symptoms will peak in the first one to two days after a drink as the body essentially goes into shock. Then it dissipates over the next three to seven days. Because that initial week (during which the body is screaming out for a drink) is so hard, residential or inpatient treatment is often advisable. If the treatment programme involves changing behavioural patterns, then it is considered wise to keep the subject in for a couple of weeks or more, since not a lot will be sinking in during that initial week or so.

With this in mind, Sporting Chance runs its 26-day residential programme eight times a year, taking in a maximum of four players per treatment episode. Everyone arrives on a Monday with the rest of their stay mapped out for them depending on their specific requirements. On the day I sat down with Colin – a Tuesday – a group of sportspeople were in their second week of treatment. That morning, they had participated in a group session with lead counsellor James West and, as we spoke, were doing shiatsu.

The next day, they would each have one-to-one sessions with West, to gauge where they were at emotionally. Because they are professional sportspeople, a space in the day is made for exercise, including tailored strength conditioning programmes. The Champney's gym is at their disposal and each afternoon contains some kind of alternative or complementary exercise. On Thursday they were going scuba diving but, as Colin said to me, 'Even though you and me might be on the same treatment programme, my content might be very different.'

Most evenings, participants would go to a 12-step meeting. Given the clinic's proximity to the capital, there's plenty to choose from within a fairly small radius, and when Joey Barton was resident they had to go to one just off the Kings Road in Chelsea's World's End. Barton's visit had come after an incident during which he had assaulted his Manchester City team-mate Richard Dunne. City chairman John Wardle was conscious of the predicament Barton was in and thought he should be sent to the clinic. If he complied, the fine that had been levied against him would be reduced.

After contact had been made, a visit was arranged and Barton was picked up from Southampton airport. The footballer described himself as 'suspicious, reticent, uncertain', and 'for the next 48 hours I veered between blandness and banality'. He even chose to eat alone, such was his frostiness. It was only on day three that the floodgates opened. He even ate with other athletes that night and began getting honest too, writing of how he had 'never related to anyone on such a deep, meaningful level'.

It was, it turned out, not a lesson fully learned. Just after Christmas 2007, Barton was charged with common assault and affray when he was caught on CCTV punching one man 20 times and breaking the teeth of another man. When the case went to trial a few months later, Barton was sentenced to six months' imprisonment. He admitted his guilt and was ordered to pay the £2,500 costs. 'I had,' Barton declared, 'stopped going to the mind gym.'

Six days after his arrest, Barton had been released on bail after Sporting Chance's Peter Kay had stressed to the judge that what he required was intensive counselling. There were onerous conditions on his being released. He would have to live with Kay and his wife for a period of time and Kay would essentially have to be at his side at all times. Additionally, Barton had to be confined indoors from 7pm until 7am every night. He was banned from drinking alcohol or even being on a licensed premises. The police even turned up unannounced at Sporting Chance to check up on him. It would be another fortnight before the judge could be convinced that he should be allowed to be available for selection again. During this period, Mike Ashley granted the use of his helicopter, an offer Barton saw as extremely generous until he later received an unexpected bill. Eventually, the terms were relaxed such that he only needed to spend one day a week with Kay and he was allowed to live in Newcastle once again, provided he was accompanied by a club-appointed security guard.

The high-profile nature of cases such as Barton's offer one explanation as to why a treatment option like Sporting Chance was needed. After all, there *isn't* a treatment centre for plumbers, as Colin had joked earlier – at least as far as I am aware! – so why one for sportspeople? 'This goes right back to Tony Adams's own experience,' Colin said. 'When he found sobriety, he was the Arsenal captain and the only doctor that he had in his life was the club doctor, and he didn't want to tell the club that he had a problem or go to his local GP. He was terrified of going into a local alcohol service. He was the England and Arsenal captain, what he wanted was a safe and private place where he could go and get help.'

'Now what he has established, we've tried to replicate. If I'm a Torquay player, you may well not know me in London but you know me in Torquay. Anonymity, confidentiality and professionalism is what we try and create for those people. There are many other good treatment providers in the country and the therapeutic content will be very similar in their treatment programme and – I'm sorry I'm using plumbers! – if we spent 20 years running a treatment programme for plumbers we'd know an awful lot about plumbers. But actually, we know an awful lot about sport. Sportspeople identify with sportspeople, an additional layer of identity: "I've faked an injury, I've sold kit, I've bet on the games I was playing in, I've been drunk when I've played." It's the identification of that career choice.'

When I pushed Colin as to whether players had come across problems with their anonymity, he quickly and firmly replied with a 'yes'. It's a tricky situation, after all, the word is right there in the name of the programme that Sporting Chance is based on, Alcoholics *Anonymous*. Colin explained that, in his eyes, it's an unavoidable (if regrettable) inevitability. People are human and they will talk. The key is that the principle is to be respected even if sometimes the letter of the tradition is breached. 'We're very protective of the players we work with and their confidentiality and anonymity. It's one of our key things, we don't do any press about players we work with – or players we haven't worked with.'

'We do find with some players, even at quite a low level, struggle when they start to go to local [12-step] meetings in as much as they are known by other people in the fellowship and people want to talk to them about football; we've even had players who've been asked for autographs or tickets.' Sometimes, a player's fear of their anonymity being broken is a real one, and sometimes it's another way of contriving to not go to meetings. 'We've had players,' Colin said, 'that have got a sponsor [essentially, a mentor in AA] and all of a sudden the sponsor is asking them for tickets to a game. You know, people are people after all, and the country loves football. So if you're playing for Mansfield you're probably big in Mansfield, so sometimes players travel out of the area to go to meetings.'

Alcoholics Anonymous's 11th tradition states: 'Our public relations policy is based on attraction rather than promotion; we need always maintain personal anonymity at the level of press, radio and films.' Put it alongside the 12th, which reads 'Anonymity is the spiritual foundation of all our Traditions, ever reminding us to place principles before personalities' in its short form, and you cannot escape the conclusion that there has been an element of creative interpretation on the part of many high-profile figures. One striking Amazon review of Tony Adams's *Sober* is titled 'This is all well and good Tony until you drink again,' and goes on to explain, 'I lost count of how many AA traditions were broken in just the first page of this book. This is all well and good Tony until you drink again, then it'll be much more than just a personal tragedy.'

Adams, for his part, seems to have been aware that this type of criticism would come – and has no doubt been levelled at him before. 'Some will criticise me for that,' he wrote, 'and some in AA have.' There would seem to be wisdom in being fairly guarded about one's methods in the first months and years of sobriety but, once a firm foundation has been established, there may be some merit in at least being open – though not evangelistic – about how one has reached that point. 'There is some of that fame but people do balance it really well,' Colin said, as we drove out of the grounds at Champney's, 'There are other very high-profile people inside sport and outside sport who are able to strike that right balance.

'Once you begin to look around there's a lot people who are in professional sport that are in recovery, living their lives via a 12-step programme, going to meetings and they become role models within their clubs and leaders within the club. It is a massive problem but it has to be said that the solution has a really positive impact beyond "I've just stopped drinking". Tony played seven years of his career sober, and in recovery, and he won more trophies in that last seven years than they won in the whole of his career before. Football became easy, he didn't even break a sweat. He was the leader he wanted to be; all aspects of our lives become improved, we change and then our world changes around us.'

The challenge for footballers – as for anyone – is that the initial stages of recovery from alcoholism require devotion of time and mental resources. The difference is that the man on the street can do it away from the focus of tens of thousands of fans in the stands and hundreds of thousands or even millions more across the globe. Nor do they have to look out for tabloid reporters or worry about being caught unawares by a long lens. Footballers have to balance those pressures with the need to devote themselves to forming the habits of a new lifestyle, which may require weeks or months away from the game. When that's done, they may need further time to get back to match fitness or may have fallen out of their manager's plans entirely.

Crucially, players will leave the clinic fit enough to play. Indeed, there have been players who have completed their treatment on Friday and played on a Saturday. They might not be match sharp in the sense that they won't have been taking part in all the drills their team-mates have, but their physical fitness should be intact. That physical side is important for their team but it's often important to a footballer's identity too. Addiction is often described (especially in 12-step-based programmes) as 'physical, mental and spiritual illness' but, as Colin puts it, 'A lot of treatment programmes don't overly respect the physical side of it, they think the physical side is just about the physical addiction.

'Sports guys need to move their body, they need to be in contact [with the ball] as part of their identity. So we will engage players in physical activity; sometimes I meet people in 12-step meetings that I go to that get over [their primary addiction] and their addiction moves to food or something like that and they're massive, so actually physical wellness, looking after yourself physically, has to be part of your recovery programme, especially for sports guys.'

How sympathetic are clubs with their players' wishes when they realise there is an issue that needs to be addressed? 'Often,' Colin told me, 'players can't get released from their contracts to come here, so we have a national network of therapists who will see people when they're still playing at their clubs, and we would say that normally that needs to be backed up with engagement with self-help fellowships such as Alcoholics Anonymous. If you are struggling with an addictive disorder or alcoholism, 45 minutes or an hour a week with a therapist is not going to solve your problem. You will need to engage with other support.'

Clubs do, of course, care about their players. Larger ones will have myriad player liaison and welfare officers who will cater to every whim of their stars; from booking holidays to dealing with parking fines. This has to be seen, though, in light of the reality that to the clubs these players are assets and are therefore treated as such. Elite level professional football players are expensive purchases. Naturally, the club will want to ensure his happiness and keep him playing well like a finely tuned piece of machinery. This is true for several reasons: firstly, if he's performing on the pitch he will be spreading their brand further and wider among their global audience; secondly, if it comes to a time when they want to sell him, this will have maximised his sell-on value.

If he leaves them at any point before he's aged 28 or 29, the board will be looking to make a profit on him. In most cases, not to do so would be a dereliction of their duty. Once the player has gone, however, that's the end of the club's formal responsibilities for him.

Likewise, the game's authorities – the FA, the leagues, the PFA – have certain responsibilities to their players and members. In the case of the PFA, these should extend beyond their playing career. In *Retired*, author Alan Gernon spoke to an individual who suggested that there were times when they fell down in this duty; it was all very well sending someone along to court with a player when he was in the dock, but where was the organisation a few years earlier when the player was begging for help with his drink problem?

The PFA has various helplines that players can ring in their hour of need, but what about intervention at earlier stages; prevention rather than cure? For many, when help arrives in a crisis, it is too late.

❧❦

'Arsenal in the Terry Neill years was as much about the social life as the football,' Kenny Sansom explained in *To Cap It All*. He earned himself the sobriquet 'Mr Chablis' during his time there, where a perception grew that the Terry Neill era side of the early 1980s were drinking so heavily and so frequently that they were not performing to the fullest of their abilities on the pitch. It is a view that Sansom, in hindsight, appears to support. 'We all have to

163

own up,' he wrote, 'to a certain amount of complacency that ran from the top down to the grass roots.'

Perry Groves's career at the club overlapped with Sansom's. 'It never struck me as being the wrong thing to do,' Groves explained to one interviewer. 'We were young lads who worked hard in training. We had to. George made us. This was a way of letting off steam and bonding as mates. It worked for us at that time.'

'I never knew I was becoming an alcoholic,' Sansom himself noted. 'I wasn't drinking any more than my team-mates.'

When Sansom's wife realised his drinking had become problematic, she went to George Graham – who had taken the Highbury hot seat in 1986 – to seek his guidance, suggesting that his problems had worsened after he had been dropped from the side. 'I'm sorry, Elaine,' he told her. 'Kenny has to help himself.'

She pleaded that others in the side had got away with similar behaviour and retained their place, but Sansom did not have the benefit of being one of the side's best players. Not any more, at least. He was also in a contract dispute with Graham, which hardly helped matters, and issued a 'sign me or sell me' warning. 'Rotting in the reserves, I would join a training session pissed – stinking rotten drunk,' he wrote. Worried that Nigel Winterburn had been brought in to replace him following an injury layoff, he begged Graham, 'You've had your piece of flesh. Now let me go.' Graham would not sell him, but instead declared, 'I am going to take the captaincy from you.' Tony Adams, his replacement, was waiting outside the office, a 28-year-old handing the armband over to a 21-year-old. Eventually, Sansom's wish to leave Arsenal was granted, but he had not reached his personal rock bottom yet. That would come when he quit professional football, his life spiralling out of control as he glugged through bottles of Chivas Regal Whisky while playing semi-professionally for Chertsey Town.

The lifestyle to which he had grown accustomed was a fading memory. Not only had the flash car gone, he no longer owned one at all. Only one thing, he thought, was holding him together. 'The booze was my mate. Wasn't it?' he wrote rhetorically. The fall from England international to non-league clogger was stark: 'Hotel rooms were booked for me, as were my flights … I thought I had it all. The downside was that I had become a pampered child who didn't have a clue how to take care of himself.' Things came to a head when Sansom was confronted by his GP, who told him in no uncertain terms that he had no future if he did not stop drinking. A call was made to Peter Kay at Sporting Chance, though Sansom himself continued to skirt around the dreaded 'A' word. Still, he headed to Champney's the following Monday after weaning off the alcohol over the weekend with the aid of medicine.

When he arrived, it was put to him that he would have to part with his mobile phone, a suggestion he did not take kindly to. Even so, he was persuaded to stay for 'a few days' before he would, he thought, be told that there was nothing wrong with him. He was given a single room, which helped, and when he passed two other sportsmen in the hallways 'instantly felt [he] would get along with them … it didn't take long for us to bond (that's what you do in rehab) and become supportive of each other'. They met at eight each morning to read from 'the Promises' in AA's Big Book and he began to learn about himself under the wing of James West, who asked him, 'Kenny, do you think it's the first glass of wine that is the problem, or, say, the seventh?' At first, when attending outside meetings of Alcoholics Anonymous, he would introduce himself simply by saying 'I'm Kenny', but on the 25th day of his stay appended the words 'and I'm an alcoholic'.

III
THE CULTURE OF A CLUB:
MANCHESTER UNITED

11.

IRISH SPIRIT, LANCASTRIAN TURF

*'Players are as fallible and as vulnerable
as the rest of us ... footballers are ordinary
mortals with ordinary mortals' weaknesses'*
– Matt Busby

*'I had worked hard. Money and fame made
me believe I was entitled.' – Tiger Woods*

NO story of booze and footballers would be
considered worthy of the name without mention
of George Best. He was *El Beatle*, the first football
celebrity; everything to excess. 'Until I came along, the press
weren't interested in what footballers did off the field,' he
said. 'I was the first player to dominate the front pages as
well as the back.'

A shy teenager when he arrived in Manchester, he
wrote of how he was 'even embarrassed to speak to the
conductor on the buses' on account of having to repeat

himself in order to be understood due to his thick Belfast brogue.

When international call-ups arrived, there was sometimes a difficulty in treating it as anything more than a boozy jaunt. 'The trips away with Ireland became like holidays,' he wrote. 'The matches, obviously, were taken seriously but the days leading up to them were just a bit of fun. We'd have a drink and a laugh, and there was quite a lot of activity "after hours".' Though Northern Ireland were not able to call on an array of stars, by 1982 they had qualified for a World Cup – *sans* Best – something which hardly strengthened his case. It was hardly going to help their fortunes if he was pissed every time he turned up.

At club level, Matt Busby was the closest thing that Best had to a father on English soil, a man who realised that the old-fashioned methods that had worked for him in the years after the Second World War would have to be adapted for the type of player – and man – Best was. Busby, born in Orbiston near Belshill, was hardly the image of a strict authoritarian. Indeed, he was on record as having said that 'bullying can only bring instant obedience and never lasting results'.

Even so, Best's recalcitrance was a shocking new turn in the swinging 60s. In the previous decade, Duncan Edwards's only sin had been to ride his bike with no lights, after which Busby, who had been an army PT instructor, told him that he was 'letting down everyone at the club'. Back then, nobody took much interest in what the players did outside the confines of the pitch, even if Jacky Blanchflower and

Tommy Taylor were known for swaying home from their regular drinking sessions. For the most part, Busby turned a blind eye; his players were local – not international – stars, earning no more than £20 a week.

It was clear when Best arrived that he was a boy extremely keen on self-improvement. Practising his craft relentlessly, he was fixated and extremely competitive. Yet evidence of what was to come off the field was to be found when the youth team went to a tournament in Zurich. One sunny afternoon, Best drank three pints of lager with David Farrar and Eddie Harrop – his first foray into this new world – and ended up throwing up out of the window of the taxi which was conveying the pale youngster back to the team's lodgings.

Busby, ensconced in a cafe opposite the entrance to the hotel, could tell his player was unwell. 'I felt like I was dying,' said Best. 'I just hoped that there wouldn't be a knock on the door and I'd open it to find the boss staring at me.' Given his slight frame, he was at greater risk of throwing up than his more developed compadres. As Farrar recalled, 'What I remember is George being sick everywhere.' In the hungover refrain of many a teenager, Best said he would never drink again. Like most teenagers, that would quickly become a broken vow – within a year he developed a taste for vodka and lemonade, lighter on his breath and with the added benefit that if caught out he could tell bosses it was flat lemonade.

Still, the descent was a long way off. This was still the 60s; televised highlights on a Saturday night – in the form of the broadcast of *Match of the Day* – had arrived in 1965 when the BBC paid £50,000 for the rights to broadcast matches from across the entire pyramid. Best was aged 19 and would go out modestly of a Saturday evening, more interested in skirt than sangria. His friend, the hairdresser Malcolm Wagner, said, 'We'd go to the cinema and then to a nightclub for an hour or two. Going out was never about the drinking then and George didn't drink much at all.' Best would turn down pints that were offered to him, informing whoever had offered it, 'I don't really drink.'

He also struck up a friendship with Mike Summerbee of Manchester City. They would meet each other off the coach of whoever had played an away game that Saturday. Summerbee had arrived in the city having already made 218 league appearances. 'Everything in Swindon closed at ten o'clock at night. Everything in Manchester was open until five o'clock in the morning,' he said. Best's problem at this time was not drinking. It was more that he did not rest: 'It was a bit daft. I was living 24 hours a day and letting myself get really run down.'

His curfew at Mrs Fullaway's – as it was for all United players, regardless of the digs they were residing in – was 10.30pm. Best did not have a key, so if he returned after his landlady had turned in for the night, he would navigate the ascent through his bedroom window via a nearby window cleaner's ladder. In the end, Mrs Fullaway relented and got a key cut, keeping Busby in the dark as to this development. When morning came, he would routinely be awoken at 7.30am by Mary Fullaway rubbing his nose. Her support was not merely practical in nature, it was emotional too. She granted him latitude for minor indiscretions because she recognised how acutely homesick he was during those earliest months in Manchester.

Outside of her house, Busby knew everything that happened in Manchester. 'If you had a glass of lager, he would get to know about it,' Best said. He knew to ignore certain reports, but warned the team, 'You can be sure, if you do anything wrong, somebody will tell me.' Unfortunately for Best, the feedback he was getting was consistent. Although it did not involve alcohol, nightclubs kept cropping up. Best was quietly talked to. Busby had a maxim: 'Private flagellation is as painful and as lastingly effective as the public variety. But it preserves the offender's dignity.' He would explain, 'Public punishment is sometimes a sop to the pride of the man who decides to inflict it.' When a player needed to be set right, he would pull them into the referee's room at Old Trafford. With Best, he had to be firm even while recognising he was different. 'One wrong way of reducing tension is to go boozing in a nightclub,' he said. 'Another is simply to stay out longer than orders permit. These methods may well take off tension, but they take the edge off performance, too. Such novelties must be stamped upon no matter whose toes are bruised.'

After being temporarily left out of the side following one such misdemeanour, Best vowed never to put 'pleasure before playing' again. Busby hoped that, as had been the case when Bobby Charlton had been similarly rebuked for drinking a single beer some years earlier, it would be a long time before Best picked up another punishment. As we know, this hope was naive. This was a different time, a freer time, a less austere era than Charlton's. Soon Best had a boutique, cutting a Gatsby-esque figure in late-1960s Manchester. Where other players washed their hair with carbolic soap, he preferred to use shampoo and dry it with a hairdryer.

The maximum wage had been abolished in 1960 when the FA were defeated in the High Court, and in 1968 Best earned £100,000 through on- and off-field activities. By 1969 he was bringing in £5,000 a week, though his actual basic salary from United would never rise above £140 a week. Before the abolition of the maximum wage, a player's earnings had been capped at £20 a week during the season and just £17 a week in the summer. At the turn of the millennium, a Premier League player over the age of 20 could count on earning an average of £8,000 a week through his club salary alone and 100 or so would be pulling in more than £1million a year from their employer.

Despite, or perhaps because of, his success, Best grew restless. 'I never stay in,' he said. 'I can't sit in the house. I can't sit down for five minutes on end. I've got to be on the move all the time. Wednesday to Saturday, it's murder. I know I've got to stay off the town and get to bed by 11. But it drives me nuts. The only thing that keeps me sane is remembering there'll be a party on Sunday and Monday and Tuesday.'

His attention would have been drawn to United's leather booklet of rules consisting of 16 pages, which contained stipulations to do with dress, kit, doctor's orders, friends, as well as cigarettes and alcohol. Entitled 'Training Rules and Playing Instructions', its 13th edict stated that 'Any player rendering himself unfit to perform his duties through drinking or any other causes will be severely dealt with.' All players possessed a pass book, explaining that they were expected to 'attend the Ground, or such other place as the directors may appoint, at 10.00 every morning (except Saturday) to undergo such training as the Manager or Trainer appointed by the Directors shall order.' They were also expected to arrive at Old Trafford 45 minutes before a home match. A preceding rule concerned smoking, explaining that it was 'strictly prohibited during training hours, and players are earnestly requested to reduce smoking to the absolute minimum on the day of a match.'

Another directive, not contained within either of these publications, probed even further into a player's personal life. It read: 'The player shall not ... live in any place which the Directors of the club may deem unsuitable.' Unmarried players were told that they were required to live in club-approved digs in order that they could receive 'proper attention and food' and stay out of mischief. Clubs' imposition into their private lives was nothing new. In 1932 Len Graham's contract at Millwall had made clear that he was not allowed to drive a car, or even be a passenger in one. Furthermore, he was barred from running or living in a pub and was required – as were his team-mates – to be indoors by 10pm each evening, or 8pm if they were injured. At training, he and his fellow Lions had to sign in and out and were not allowed to depart at the end of their rigours without permission. Similarly, during a previous era Hull City players were forbidden from attending dances after Tuesday evening unless they had sought prior permission or were accompanied by a chaperone from the club. Operating a like-minded regime, officials at Brentford had declared that 'some players have to be saved from themselves'.

This was not a practice confined to these clubs. In his autobiography, *Spotlight on Football*, Peter Doherty fondly recalled his time in accommodation at Blackpool before the Second World War: 'On the Friday before a home game, we would all report at a local hotel for tea. [Manager] Sandy MacFarlane would treat us to a show, and then order us to bed about ten o'clock, rather like a Victorian father. Often if we were spending the Friday night in the digs, Jack Charles [manager of the reserves] would call round to make sure that we intended to have an early night.'

Sweetly, he seems to have had little interest in any vice other than larking about with his mates. 'With me in digs were Sam and Tommy Jones, and we quickly became firm pals. We neither drank nor smoked, and none of us had a girl: an occasional visit to the pictures suited us perfectly when we wanted an evening out. We were inseparable, and the rest of the lads at Bloomfield Road quickly got into the habit of calling us the "Three Musketeers". They would shout, "They don't drink, they don't smoke and they don't go with women. What do they live for?" We three knew the answer: it was football.' A man named Peter Doherty focussing on his art, who would have thought it?

A similar situation existed at Wolves in the 1950s too. Stan Cullis explained the process his players undertook in a subsequent autobiography: 'As soon as he arrives at Wolverhampton, he will be met at the station by George Noakes, the club's chief scout, or by one of his assistants, and taken to his new home. His landlady will become a "second mother" for she will probably have been on the club's list for several years. We know that her house will provide exactly the right atmosphere for a young footballer, that she will insist that the young man keeps good hours and she will provide him with good food.' Incredibly, one Wolves player, Billy Wright, ended up happily residing with his landlady for 20 years before meeting his wife. United's own setup at this time involved two big houses being knocked into a single dwelling, meaning one landlady could be responsible for up to 20 young men at once, with Bobby Charlton and Duncan Edwards among those passing through its hallways.

Wolves, it should be noted, seemed to be unusually forward-thinking even before this era. Before World War Two, they employed a qualified psychiatrist for the benefit of their playing squad, something which many managers would have dismissed as excessively touchy-feely even 50 years later. When Tottenham appointed one in the 1980s, a newspaper ran with the headline: 'White Coats at White Hart Lane'. When the BBC's *Radio 5 Live* had enquired as to which clubs utilised a psychologist in the 1990s, only one – Derby County – admitted to doing so. Many others certainly did but would either deny it or employ them under euphemistic titles.

❧✿❧

Let's return once again to the streets of Manchester. Before Best's explosion into superstardom, he had a small circle of friends consisting of Danny Bursk, Eddie 'Freight Train'

Hindle, a clothes company rep, Malcolm Mooney, who was in the same trade, Frank Evans, who would go on to become a bullfighter in Spain, plus, of course, the elder statesman Summerbee. Together, they were known as 'The Chaps'. Best had tried to befriend some of his married team-mates off the field, but 'thought none of them liked [him] because no one suggested going out'. This being the 1960s, pubs were not actually open all that much, shutting after the lunchtime session for several hours. When they were taking orders, a pint would set you back two shillings, meaning you could get comfortably drunk for a pound.

He and Summerbee would go to Arturo's of a Saturday night, a popular restaurant where Busby and other officials also ate. They would stay for only 15 minutes or so – a charade – in an attempt to convince the management that they were sensible young men. Nobody was fooled. 'We'd always go and say goodbye,' Summerbee said, 'and be perfect gentlemen. The wives were always telling us to take care of ourselves and we always promised we would. The managers knew where we'd be going and why, and there was never any bother about it provided you didn't turn up the worse for wear on a Monday morning.'

Best would soon become acutely aware of his star power and began to cultivate it. The time he turned up on that beach in Estoril with the wide brimmed hat, the moment he became *El Beatle*, is seen by many biographers as a turning point. For all involved, there was simply no blueprint; this was completely uncharted territory. He was getting 10,000 letters delivered in hessian sacks from adoring fans every single week. He had become a willing partner in his dance with celebrity, and of being looked at in the street he described as a 'marvellous feeling'. Later, he would rent a flat in the city centre with Summerbee, while officially still living under the purview of his doting landlady. His bolthole allowed him the freedom to indulge his late-night excesses away from the prying eyes of the club.

The flat had just one bedroom, so their weekend stays involved a contest to secure this prize, often having asked the cab drivers to take a non-linear route so that visiting women would not know exactly where they were. Nights would end in a shebeen – an establishment operating outside of licensing hours – quite often Clifton Grange, which was owned by Phil Lynott's – of Thin Lizzy – mother. Best said, 'The parties would go on all night. It really did become an institution ... they packed to the doors every night, almost. The time I spent there probably did more to me as an athlete than any other single factor.' Not that he knew it at the time. He could not imagine not living like this forever, remarking that he could not 'contemplate reaching 40. I think I'd rather die before being that old – peacefully in my sleep.' He chose not to think about it: 'I went on going out every night and drinking. I thought it wouldn't catch up with me ... I could get totally pissed and it didn't seem to matter ... I could handle hangovers then.'

At this point, Busby tried to look the other way, hoping Best would settle down soon. The tabloid press was not what it would go on to become, so there was a certain amount of latitude to do so. To him it was all quite incomprehensible; he was a man of a different time and he did not have the answers – as hard as he tried – when it all began to unravel for Best a few years later. He tried all sorts of approaches, including telling him to get married. This was a notion that had the backing of Best's mother, who would ultimately die as the result of a decade of her own drinking. She said, 'I'm sure that's the basis for most of his troubles. He has the fancy girlfriends. I'm not talking about them. I'm talking about the ordinary girl with her feet on the ground, who would cook for him and care for him.'

By now, the boy from east Belfast had built a large white house, Que Sera, just outside the city. His residence became a symbol of his situation with armies of ardent admirers camped out on the lawn. 'It was a disaster. I dreaded going home. I was a prisoner,' he said. The idea, never likely to happen, was that his parents would eventually cross the Irish Sea and live with him. He was, he writes, a 'lonely, mixed-up Irishman who couldn't come to terms with what he wanted from life'.

The loneliness, depressiveness and riddle of contradictions that we associate with the fantasy of what Best represented had become deep-rooted. His aversion to confrontation – with himself, his managers, his demons – was plain for all to see. He would talk out of both sides of his mouth, duplicity having become a prerequisite of keeping everyone happy and his boozy lifestyle ticking along unimpeded. His friend Malcolm Mooney remarked that 'he told lies beautifully'. He was good at showing contrition, whether sincere or not. 'I used to sit in front of him and nod yes,' he said of his stern chats with Busby. 'He talked quietly to me. He screamed at me. He suspended me.

He fined me. He put an arm round me. He did everything humanly possible.'

Nevertheless, Busby felt warm towards him in an almost fatherly way, despite a seemingly total inability to get through to him. 'I am sure that he wanted to be different and that he always intended to keep his promises. But he lacked self-control. With him it was a promise today broken tomorrow ... There was always a next time, another disaster.' This paternal instinct may have caused Busby to persist with attempting to 'fix' Best for longer than was sensible. 'I have to sit back and remember he is a grown man,' he said. A man from a stoical era, in exasperation he told Best that he should 'talk to someone', but Best was dismissive of the suggestion of psychiatry. When it was suggested he restrict his socialising, Best replied, 'I don't want to. I don't want to be like everyone else.'

Busby, who had not held a top job in football when he became United manager in the bombed wreckage of the Second World War, had a way of dealing with his players, 'You always felt embarrassed that a man like that should give you a dressing down,' Paddy Crerand said. 'He'd never demean you. He'd make you feel a bit ashamed you'd done something that wasn't proper.' By the time Busby had moved upstairs to the Old Trafford boardroom, Best's life was beginning to take a turn towards the absurd. A driven man, he was nevertheless temperamentally unable to take on board the advice of others, especially those he considered inferior. On one occasion, he brought a woman to his room the night before a match in defiance of new boss Wilf McGuinness, knowing that he was too important within the Old Trafford ecosystem to be completely frozen out. The next day, he would miss an easy chance in the team's match versus Leeds and United went on to lose the replay.

His team-mates were growing tired of his exploits but, as Paddy Crerand explained, 'The trouble was, he just agreed with you and said he'd change, he'd learned his lesson and it would all be different. It never was.' Not that they were not protective of their oftentimes wayward companion. Crerand would go on to punch the patron of a nightclub who had bad-mouthed Best. Sometimes, when it all got too much, Best would simply hide away from the intrusion, bolting the door of the actress Sinead Cusack's flat, or flying to Marbella. After one disappearing act, Best was sent to live in the Crerand family home, lasting all of five days in an environment not conducive to his lifestyle. Another time, Crerand had driven to the airport to stop Best fleeing the country. He went anyway, reappearing 17 days later. 'I wasn't thinking of the matches at all,' Best said as he turned 25. 'I was fed up with everything – and everyone – around me.'

The European Cup marked the peak of Best's four-year footballing pomp, one that never reached its ceiling. Two years later in 1970, United were a club in crisis. Best could not deal with not being The Best. Perhaps the signs were there even on the night of the European Cup win in 1968, of which Best's memories were patchy. 'I went out and got drunk,' said Best, piecing the night together through the recollections of others, even forgetting how he had left Wembley. 'Almost everything was a blank. I don't know what I did,' he said. Arriving after midnight in a taxi at Jackie Glass's flat, she remembered that, 'He seemed drained of emotion.' It should have been the start of something great, the first of many. But it was not. He felt it as soon as pre-season began after the summer: 'I was only warming up ... I was hungry ... I was someone who wasn't going to reach my peak for another seven years.'

United had imploded. 'Instead of revolving around me, the team now depended on me and I lacked the maturity to handle it,' Best said, adding, 'We were getting worse. It got so bad that I didn't want to wake up in the mornings ... We were losing and I felt this terrible emptiness.' Best demanded that the team be rebuilt with him as the centrepiece. Busby told him he was not responsible. 'Make me captain and I will be responsible,' he replied.

'Because I was being treated as if I was irresponsible, I started behaving irresponsibly off the park. I was a rebel,' Best explained. It seems an unlikely explanation – an excuse – for behaviours that had long pre-existed this moment. 'I couldn't face simply being a very good player,' he moaned, seeking special treatment. 'If someone has a talent or a gift or is different ... they have to be treated differently.' Expounding on this self-exculpatory philosophy, he continued: 'If I was in charge of a team and I had the greatest player in the world and he chose on days to turn up with no socks on I would let him do it if he was performing on the field.' He was, in truth, seeking licence to be George Best.

When he perceived team-mates to be excessively buttoned up, he scorned them. One of the targets of his ire was Bobby Charlton, with whom he no longer got on. 'They've been great,' he said of his team-mates, 'all except one. I'm not saying who he is, but his name is Bobby Charlton … I wish I could hear him say fuck just once.'

In line with most observers, he guessed that the booze took over 'around 1970 or 1971'. The way he paints it, he had the weight of the whole club on his shoulders after that, and he simply could not cope, even if the problem would not become glaringly obvious for another few years. Busby's right-hand man, the Welshman Jimmy Murphy, called Best 'the hardest trainer I've ever seen', able to sweat out the alcohol in training, but only for as long as he was able to rouse himself to turn up at the Cliff. When the signs of his excess began to show in his pallor, he grew a beard in part to hide the blotches which marked his skin. A United director asked Busby if he ought to suggest it be shaved off, only to be told, 'If you can guarantee to me that if he takes off his beard he will be a better player, then he will have it taken off tomorrow.'

The beard, it scarcely needs to be said, was just a physical manifestation of a deeper malaise. In time, the thickness of the beard became a barometer for his emotional state; as it grew, he became sicker and less punctual. After a while, he would sometimes not show up to training at all: 'I was getting home when [United] were reporting for training. It got to the stage where I couldn't get up to go … I was too embarrassed to let the lads smell drink on me.' This became a regular occurrence and he decided he would resign once again, his thunder stolen when the club fired him instead. 'I'd have got smashed the night before and I was still pissed. I'd hear Paddy Crerand say that I stank like a brewery.'

For Best, it was a lonely era. 'Drink became my company instead of people,' he wrote. 'Physically and mentally, I went beyond my limits.' Best developed a beer gut, and when he 'quit' United boss Frank O'Farrell decided that pursuing him would be counterproductive. Sacking him would be too expensive, though, given that he was probably worth well in excess of £500,000. Six weeks later, Best returned and O'Farrell was asked what he thought Best's prospects were. 'You know me,' he said, 'an eternal optimist.' More candidly, he later declared, 'If Busby couldn't handle George, how could I?' After Busby's house was suggested as his new lodgings, it was at this point he spent a short while living with Crerand, having gained two stone in weight.

On another occasion, he had informed O'Farrell he was with his family in Belfast, a story which fell down because O'Farrell was himself with Dickie and Ann at the time George had claimed to be there. The former Leicester manager resorted to quoting Proverbs 24:16, 'for though the righteous fall seven times, they rise again' at his player, as Best desperately sought to justify himself and his actions.

As United slid further, Tommy Docherty was brought in to instil some order. When he arrived, Best was in the middle of another self-imposed exile from the Cliff, holed up in the Brown Bull pub, even sleeping there on a filthy mattress on occasion. The Brown Bull, owned by an American, had been an unremarkable watering hole until Best began to frequent it, after which it became popular with Manchester's high society. Famously, Matt Busby found its name difficult to comprehend and would moan about the 'Brown Cow' and other mangled versions of its name.

When thrombosis hospitalised Best, it was Busby who was dispatched to talk some sense into him. Playing the good cop this time, he coaxed Best into thinking a return had been his own idea. 'I've missed the game more than I thought I would. I would like to think that the drinking problems I had and the depressions they caused are behind me,' Best said.

It was another false dawn. The winger simply was not at the races. On New Year's Day 1974 he arrived for a match against QPR clearly hungover. A few days later, he turned up late for an FA Cup fixture versus Plymouth Argyle. The story goes that he turned up at 2.35pm to be told by Docherty, 'Rather than thinking about playing football, you should be thinking about being breathalysed.' His name had already been scratched off the team sheet at 2.15pm. When he was sent home by Docherty, under whom he had made a total of 12 appearances, this time it was finally over.

'Bringing him back,' Docherty said, 'was a disaster. He was more trouble than he was worth.' Best was suspended and put on the transfer list. 'He was subject to no real discipline, and by that I mean sensible discipline. He did what he wanted and got away with murder.' This might seem dramatic, but Docherty had previously fined and dropped eight players at Chelsea for missing a curfew on an away trip in Blackpool, nixing a slim chance of winning the league title. 'I suppose one could say that I forsook what chance we had of winning the championship on a matter of principle,' he said. 'However, I felt I had to make a stand.'

Staying at the Norbreck Castle hotel, several of Docherty's players at Chelsea – among them George

Graham and Terry Venables! – had become bored and decided to venture into the city centre. Their escape act was undone, however, by the night porter who had grassed them up to the manager. After finishing his meal, he had gone to confront his players, who had just made it back. He discovered each of them in bed, still dressed in their suits. Without them, Chelsea lost 6-2.

In this manner, Docherty had professionalised the Manchester United side once more. His regimen meant that they stayed in a hotel – Mottram Hall, near Macclesfield – the night before home matches, which was an innovation for United. The loudest voice during those nights was Docherty's own, lubricated by the Scotch he enjoyed. Yet when Louis Edwards took a controlling interest in the club, the hotels were seen as a frivolity too far and – to Docherty's chagrin – the expense was struck from the budget.

❧

Recollections and anecdotes about Best can – and have – filled entire books. Best himself attributed some of his personal difficulties to threats on his life purported to have originated from the IRA, which certainly coincided with his descent from the heights of the game. Writing in *Blessed*, Best noted that, 'I was under enormous pressure as it was and having enough problems just keeping my life together, without that, and it wasn't just the threat that bothered me. It was the effect I knew it would have on my family. They were living with the Troubles on a daily basis, which was hard enough for them.' Indeed, Best's mother, Ann, had barely touched a drop of alcohol before her 40th birthday but was dead from its effects by the age of 54.

Best is one of the hardest of our subjects to understand or even sympathise with. There is no redemptive arc; there were periods of abstinence, yes, but then there is the liver transplant and pouring drink on top of it, before his eventual death in November 2005. Some of this difficulty may also stem from the mawkishness that has built up around his legend: the way that every aspect of his life was romanticised, every wrongdoing explained away as the actions of a misunderstood genius. The bare fact is that his career was essentially over by the age of 25, frittered away because he had lost his love of the game as his life became filled with alcohol. In a sense, that probably contributes to his iconic status; his further forays in football were largely away from the limelight and did not serve to blemish the reputation that had been built at Old Trafford in the 60s. Once that door had been closed, the story is largely played out in west London wine bars and increasingly obscure locations as Best's footballing motivations became mercenary.

The line between Best's private and public personas become blurred beyond recognition. He played up to the latter. 'Drink changed my personality,' he said. 'Everybody, it seems, was happy to drink with George Best, and who was I to disappoint them? It didn't take too many drinks to become the George Best they wanted to drink with. The other George Best wouldn't have interested them much.' He could no longer imagine himself being anything other than this caricature. 'What happens is that you get caught up in a myth … to some extent, there's always been a need to put on an act for people, if only to protect myself.' Though he had the resources to do as he pleased, he mused that 'I sometimes think I would like to be an ordinary bloke' and that rather than help he wanted 'understanding'.

It was only in 1981, aged 35, that he first admitted that the nature of his drinking amounted to alcoholism. Two years previously, he had maintained, 'I've never considered myself an alcoholic. I don't wake up gasping for a drink.' There were treatment episodes, such as the one at Vespers in the United States. But he still saw himself as different from those around him, yet to reach a rock bottom. He was discharged after completing 18 of the 30 days. 'I was a fraud. I faked it,' he said, vowing not to drink for a year.

When he returned for a second stint, this time he was serious and collected a chip to mark a period of continuous sobriety, common among AA fellowships. Yet it was not to last. His days as an itinerant player for hire were drawing to a close. When they did, any limitations on his lifestyle disappeared too. 'When I was playing,' he said, 'I wasn't going out deliberately to drink myself into oblivion. After I stopped playing, I did.' Drinking, in and of itself, had become a competition.

'I don't like the idea of people drinking more than me,' he explained, 'so I am usually the last man standing. It's not easy for me to walk away … If my pals drank 20 pints, I'd have to have 21. If they went home at 4am, I went home at 4.30am. Instead of having six or seven drinks I'd have ten drinks and then a dozen drinks.' He wondered whether he was, on some level, deliberately exposing himself to dangerous situations in order that somebody else would force him into doing something about it. The problem was, as he succinctly put it, 'When you're drinking, nothing else but that matters.'

When he had been granted that reprieve by the replacement of his own ravaged liver, there was another vow never to drink again. He was in trouble less than a year later after fighting with a reporter outside a pub near his home in Reigate. Reportedly, he had told his then wife Alex, 'I'm sorry. I just can't help myself.' Before the transplant, he had been given three months to live and, though it gave him a few more years, eventually the drink finished him off.

At first, drink had been a way to overcome his innate shyness – 'I might loosen up sufficiently to chat to one or two people' – then a way to deal with the adulation and the loneliness that brought about, a mechanism to forget what once was and could have been. At the end, he simply could not stop, telling one interviewer, 'At seven in the morning I am gasping for a drink.'

In his dying days, Best reportedly had a copy of AA's Big Book close to hand, a message on his hospital bed beamed out to the world 'DON'T DIE LIKE ME'. Even Antabuse, a drug which produces extreme nausea if alcohol is consumed alongside it, could not help him stop. Nor could the death of his mother, or the end of two marriages, or the destruction of his relationship with his son Calum. In the end, it was a lung infection which had spread to his kidneys which meant he saw out his final weeks in London's Cromwell hospital. Drink had finally taken the final thing from him: his life.

12.

LIQUID ASSETS

MANY clubs which had benefitted from the ecclesiastical assistance referenced earlier in this book during their formative days would go on to shed these links to the men of the cloth a few short years later. These ties were discarded, in many cases, when they became associated with large local breweries. United's cross-city rivals Manchester City were one such side, transforming from a 'church' team as St Mark's (West Gorton) to forging a partnership with a brewery by the name of Chesters.

The church was witness to the deprivation and social problems in their district of Manchester, described by no less than Friedrich Engels as a 'girdle of squalor'. St Mark's had set up a number of informal social institutions and it's thought that the impetus for a cricket team sprang out of one of the working men's meetings which had been organised by the vicar's daughter, Anna Connell. That cricket team had wondered how to occupy their vacant winter months and football offered the answer. The football team was born on 13 November 1880 when it took to the field in a friendly against a Baptist church from nearby Macclesfield in a 12 versus 12 match, the numbers boosted in all probability to ensure that everyone who wanted to participate was able to. This was, after all, the decade in which football would become a mass movement rather than a preserve of elite private schools.

A few years after its founding, the influence of the White Cross Army on St Mark's, and in turn its football team, would be clearly evident. This non-denominational purity movement had come into being in 1883 under the stewardship of a philanthropist by the name of Ellice Hopkins with the backing of the Bishop of Durham. At the time, Manchester was a renowned stronghold of the organisation which was based on the widespread temperance leagues of this era. It seems that kit was donated to the footballers by a key church figure, consisting of a black shirt with a large white cross on its front.

Before long the club was going by the name of Ardwick FC, and Stephen Chesters Thompson, local councillor and scion of the Chesters brewing family, became a key figure in the footballing boardroom. The club was headquartered at the Hyde Road Hotel, a licensed establishment which was tied to the Chesters business. The team played on ground behind that same premises in a densely populated district, one in which the brewing firm had a large number of pubs. As well as that, the brewery was the exclusive supplier to the bars within the perimeter of the ground itself. The land was not ideally suited to football, boxed in by railway lines as it was and necessitating Billy Meredith running across a plank to take corners. Nevertheless, a number of other pub chain proprietors, their hostelries concentrated in west Manchester, soon joined Chesters Thompson on City's board. Its chairman, John Chapman, owned several pubs too.

Despite its locational shortcomings, Chesters financed construction of a grandstand for 1,000 people at this location in 1888 and helped the club purchase some big-name players as they put themselves forward for membership of the Football League. Their entry to this new competition was based far more on the club's potential than its actual standing and achievements up to this point. With an eye to capitalising on this, the shareholders created a limited company: Manchester City.

It was all a long way from its humble roots as an offshoot of a parish church cricket team. When Manchester City proposed vacating their Hyde Road ground for pastures new some years later, Chesters were not pleased. They had spent good money on City only for them to attempt to leave once a fan base (and, for the brewery, a customer base) had been cultivated. When they did move to a new venue, it was – ironically – on Maine Road, renamed as such from its original moniker of Dog Kennel Lane by members of the local branch of the temperance movement who had taken inspiration from the 1853 Maine law prohibiting alcohol in the American state.

In April 1891 Ardwick had beaten Newton Heath 1-0 in the Manchester Cup Final. This was a big deal, since their neighbourhood rivals had been in every final since its inception and Ardwick were previously regarded as a minnow. Their victory here meant that they were considered a viable candidate to join the expanded Football League in 1892, in the newly created 12-team Second Division, with the top tier growing to 16 sides. Among those were Newton Heath, later to become Manchester United.

At this time, Ardwick were the better supported of the two outfits, although this did not mean they were immune to financial pressures. The club almost lost their Hyde Road home when their landlord proposed closing the entrance by the Hyde Road Hotel with the club apparently behind on its rent. The logistical challenges, even before the threat of this closure, meant that Ardwick's players had actually walked along a pathway beneath a railway arch to reach the pitch after they had prepared for the game.

Chesters – who owned the ground, if not the land it sat on – invested £2,500, financing repairs and constructing its own bars within the ground. They could not countenance that it might all be for nothing and persuaded the railway company (whose line actually ran through the ground) to keep the entrance open for the rest of the season on the proviso that they – rather than the club – would ultimately be responsible for the lease. Instead, they sublet it back to the club in 1894.

It was in this year that the club became Manchester City, taking on the motto 'Even in our own ashes live our wonted fire'. Chesters provided capital to grow this new entity, a limited company with the aim of becoming a powerful force on the burgeoning football scene. A move away to Belle Vue had been mooted, but the club was persuaded to remain at their Hyde Road venue, where ground rent could not increase for another four years. In turn, Chesters contributed to further improvements, including a new Fulham pageant stand which would hold 4,000 fans undercover in a ground that could now house a total of 28,000 spectators. It was not just fans who experienced these new luxuries; the players benefitted from the newly installed Turkish and Russian baths. Eventually, in 1917, City would reclaim the ground for themselves, long after Chesters had left an indelible mark on the club's DNA.

Their intra-city rivals Newton Heath had developed their own links to the alcohol industry when the club's captain, Harry Stafford, sought the monetary backing of John Henry Davies, head of Manchester Brewing Company. Davies had started his own journey to becoming a brewing impresario by acquiring the Derby Arms in Salford. As he accumulated greater wealth, he used this to purchase shares in breweries including the John William Lees brewery (which owned Oldham's Boundary Park), Walker & Homfray's (later taken over by Boddingtons) and the Manchester Brewery Company.

It had all come about in unsavoury circumstances. In 1900 more than 6,000 people had been poisoned by beer tainted with arsenic. Manchester was particularly hard hit when 70 people died as a result of the contamination. Davies was ruthless: the share price of all the affected breweries fell precipitously, and while Davies acknowledged this drop he suspected that sales of beer would not take a long-term hit. He bought up shares across the board and the breweries which were not affected saw their share prices shoot up. Davies had an interest in those, too. For him, it was a win-win situation.

Newton Heath's foundation had originated within the carriages of the Lancashire and Yorkshire Railway company. The company employed hundreds of men, but life expectancy in the 'Little Ireland' area from which it drew its human resources was as low as 17 years in 1850. Alcohol was a form of escape from the grinding realities of everyday life, and around 25 per cent of working-class wages were spent on getting drunk. The railway company, through its dining room committee, sought to find a less destructive solution and instigated 'classes of improvement' for their employees. These would often consist of team games to counteract the ill-effects of boozing. Rugby was an option, but the powers that be deemed football a more gentlemanly, Corinthian pursuit, as well as one less likely to result in serious injury.

The first pitch was laid over a former clay pit by a railway line in Monsall, conveniently situated on the North Road near to the company's base. During their second season, the players used a room in the Three Crowns pub on Oldham Road as a changing facility though by the time the club joined the Football League for the 1892/93 season, it had moved to a new ground on Bank Street.

Less than a decade later, in January 1902, the wolf was at the door. The club had debts amounting to £2,670 (about £280,000 in today's money) and its own president, owed £242 17s 10d, had gone to court seeking a winding-up order. Things were so bad that the receiver had padlocked the gate at their Bank Street ground and captain Harry Stafford, their full-back and a boilermaker by trade, took it upon himself to carry out fundraising efforts to save the ailing entity. Initial attempts at St James Hall proved to be of limited success, raising just enough money for the team to travel to be drubbed 4-0 by Bristol City and hire a field so they could play a home fixture against Blackpool, which they lost 1-0.

This is where Stafford's dog, Major, enters the scene. The stories vary, with one involving his canine companion disappearing from the aforementioned church hall along with the collecting tin that was attached to him. Another version has him taking his pet to a dog show. Yet another tale about the fundraising efforts involves patrons betting on a drunk goat. Nevertheless, it's agreed that Major was responsible for his meeting John Henry Davies in a pub which belonged to the Manchester Brewery.

Davies, bestowed of bushy eyebrows and a big moustache, owned the Manchester brewery, which, in turn, owned the pub they had met in. One thing led to another, and by the end of the evening Davies had agreed to invest £500 into Newton Heath alongside a number of other businessmen contributing similar amounts. Between them, these businessmen took responsibility for the large debts of the floundering footballing operation – on the brink of liquidation – that would become Manchester United Football Club. The club was, essentially, run as a sister company to the alcohol business: four of its six first directors were employees from the brewery and, eventually, even the manager J.J. Bentley got his pay cheque from their coffers.

Davies knew football could be used for profit. He gave Harry Stafford a pub in Ancoats to manage and discovered that having a footballer behind the bar was a licence to print money. According to one source, he also gave Billy Meredith the funds to start his famous sports equipment shop in St Peter's Square. Meredith, who had re-founded the players' union in 1907 in the era of a £4-a-week maximum wage, would later become a publican too, although he was an infrequent drinker himself.

It was in 1915 that Meredith took over a pub on the Stockport Road. That was close to City's ground, and by 1930 he had become the landlord of the Stratford Road Hotel, which became known colloquially as 'Billy Meredith's'. His brother was a Methodist minister (their parents had been of the primitive variety) and would only cross the threshold of the establishment singing temperance songs. Meredith's own near-sobriety had come in handy during his playing days, not least when looking after his team-mate William Gillespie. Often drunk, this necessitated his wages being held onto by Meredith. This was not totally unusual among the City team, and before big games they would often be taken to the seaside for a few days to keep them out of the pub and under supervision.

Back in the west of the city, in 1909, it was Davies again who provided the £60,000 sum required to finance the purchase of land upon which to construct Old Trafford. Housing 77,000 fans, it boasted state-of-the-art facilities for its time, including a billiard room, gym, laundry, massage room and a tea room. Such lavish facilities for players and staff were rare at the time; only recently had White Hart Lane acquired its own social club so that players could congregate within refined surroundings, including two fireplaces, two billiard tables and only a small bar.

To the possible chagrin of one or two of Roy Keane's ancestors, the newly built Old Trafford also contained 750 upholstered theatre-style tip-up seats for local dignitaries. In fact, the arrangement involved the club leasing the land from the brewery, a situation which the FA eventually became unhappy with as it was thought the club were gaining an unfair financial advantage due to the generous terms of the deal. Such was the extent of his investment that many of Davies's loans were not fully repaid until after the Second World War.

Upon taking control seven years previously, he was also the instigator of fresh colours – red and white – replacing the existing blue and white kit and suggested a new name for the club should be sought, since they no longer played on the Heath. After suggestions of Manchester Central and Manchester Celtic were discarded, a supporter is said to have come up with a name, and – reflecting their desire to be a club for the whole of the city – they became Manchester United in the spring of 1902.

13.

SINK OR SWIM

WHEN Ron Atkinson arrived at Old Trafford 80 years later, standard operating procedure was that any issues among the playing staff would be sorted out over a few drinks under the watchful eye of Bryan Robson. Norman Whiteside, just 17, announced his presence on the footballing scene the following year when United won the League Cup and Atkinson suggested that the young man have a beer to celebrate. That was nothing unusual for the manager, who said, 'I never wanted training to be a prisoner of war camp. I wanted to see players with a bit of bounce, a bit of zip. I don't see it that if someone's having a laugh or a joke, they're not switched on ... I like players to have enthusiasm.'

Although embraced by the majority, this method of generating 'enthusiasm' was not one that was appreciated by every member of the dressing room. Chief among the sceptics was Frank Stapleton, who had arrived from Arsenal: 'It was the same set of guys who used to go out all the time,' he told author and *United We Stand* editor Andy

Mitten. 'We would train on Tuesday morning and then be off until Thursday. The lads would go out after training and would turn in at all hours of the morning ... I believe that if they had done it less then we could have achieved more with the quality of players that we had.'

Not all of his team-mates agreed. Scotsman Arthur Albiston didn't see an issue. 'We were a football club,' he said to Mitten, 'not a social club. We had a responsibility to the supporters. We liked a laugh and night out, but there wasn't a drinking culture different from any other club.' Albiston had been one of United's drinking crew until 1987 when, at the urging of his wife, he knocked it on the head entirely.

Robson had apparently told Atkinson, 'Gaffer, I can't get any of them to go out,' shortly after he had been signed from West Brom but it would not be long before their lock-ins at the Park – Paddy McCrerand's pub – became a common occurrence. Yet it would be wrong to say that all of them were out on the piss every night. During the season it was largely confined to Saturday nights and Sunday lunchtimes. Sometimes Tuesday would be a drinking day too – and this might slip into a Wednesday – but it was the 1980s and none of this was unusual in English football.

Despite dissenting voices like Stapleton's, drink was becoming a major talking point in discussions of Manchester United once again, in a way that had not been the case since the days of George Best. Atkinson was seen as a lax supervisor, disinclined to impose discipline. Kevin Moran, who spent a decade at United, later said in conversation with Mitten, 'Our drinking was never, ever frowned upon or clamped down on. I can never remember Ron calling us in and having a go at us over drinking during the week.' It was an accepted part of the game. Moran, though, maintained that the perception that the team were constantly boozing was inaccurate. 'Thursday night, I could go to the pub for a couple,' he said. 'But I'd never kick on after that, maybe two or three drinks, that would be it.' Back then, players at all clubs would regularly have a few pints on a Thursday night – a day and a half was seen as more than adequate recovery time.

Until Alex Ferguson arrived, they had had a manager who was intensely relaxed about it too. Bryan Robson would let Big Ron know he was taking some of the players out and that was that. When fit, the trio of McGrath, Whiteside and Robson were probably the best players he had, so there was a certain amount of leeway to be found.

Frank Stapleton thought that the team could have done more: 'Everyone keeps talking about Liverpool being just as bad for drink and I don't really believe it. I mean I'm sure they had drinkers, but I don't think they went on huge binges … towards the end it got really, really bad. Players were just running riot, more or less doing what they wanted.' There may have been peer pressure but, as Stapleton made clear, 'It was always down to yourself how much you drank.' He saw the light training regime, which granted the players so much free time – in contrast to his spell at Arsenal – as being unhelpful for a number of the squad, not least McGrath: 'I think someone even stronger than him would have been lured into the drink culture … It didn't help Paul's situation. Actually, it probably made it a lot worse.'

Goalkeeper Gary Bailey's recollection concurred on the theme of underachievement: 'The drinking culture was a problem, no question,' he said to Mitten. 'It wasn't a problem for people like Bryan Robson, who enjoyed the drinking and still performed perfectly well. But it created a culture that other players were not comfortable with ... I bumped heads constantly with the "you cope or piss off home" approach.' Bailey had essentially been bullied by his team-mates earlier in his career, 'It was bad when my team-mates turned on me when my form wasn't good ... I ended up having treatment for ulcers because of the tension of trying to survive this tough environment.' This only stopped when he very deliberately went in hard on Martin Buchan in training, sending a message. Bailey saw the culture under Dave Sexton at United as being responsible for the departures of Andy Ritchie and Nikola Jovanovic. The manager was not directly involved in the treatment meted out to them, yet he had failed to clamp down on it.

Bailey, who was close with Stapleton, would often act as something of a minder to the other players, telling bouncers when the team were on tour, 'If there's any trouble with us don't touch the players, but come to me and I'll sort them out,' and even warning his own team-mates, 'You cause trouble and I'll take you out.' He had tried to match them drink for drink on one occasion, only serving to confirm his belief that he was not cut out for it, '[...] Robbo arranged a session in the Four Seasons in Hale. I thought, "I'm going to try and be one of the lads. I can fight now and I'm playing well, so I'll give it my best shot." Well, they drank so quickly – Robbo, Norman, Paul McGrath and Kevin Moran – that

I had to stop them buying me drinks. I got to pint number four after an hour before saying, "Please guys, I can't keep up. I need a break."' He went home to sleep it off during the afternoon, awaking at 6pm, returning to meet the drinking gang who were by now on their 16th pint. He had one more with them before returning home once again, leaving them to reach pint number 20.

Among the players' favourite haunts were The Griffin in Bowdon, Little B in Brooklands, the aforementioned Four Seasons and Paddy Crerand's pub in Altrincham. 'We'd all meet in Paddy's pub,' Gordon McQueen recalled, talking to Mitten. 'It was a place ahead of its time. They had continental hours there long before 24-hour licensing.' The Park had opened at the start of the 1982 World Cup in Spain, a place that the players could drink without the intrusion they would have to deal with elsewhere. When one regular alerted the powers that be at Old Trafford to Robson's repeated visits to Crerand's pub, the grass was smoked out and received a punch across the face for his troubles and reportedly even had to leave the area.

'Ron had the approach,' Bailey informed Mitten, 'that if you got up in the morning and did the business you were OK. I didn't agree. I felt that heavy drinking would do you long-term damage. If it didn't damage Robbo then it certainly damaged Norman Whiteside and Paul McGrath's careers.' Even Atkinson himself has come to believe that United would have treated a player other than McGrath more strictly: 'They would not have tolerated it,' he wrote, 'but because it was Paul and because he had a problem, they let it go.'

Another player firmly within the moderate camp was the Dutchman Arnold Muhren, who 'was quite surprised at the drinking culture. In Holland we'd have a drink after a game on a Sunday evening. But you can't do that too often and at United there was a couple of players who went drinking during the week as well, which is not the right way to do things. On Sundays there was not a lot to do in England and a lot of players went to the pub.' Chatting to Mitten, he credited his self-control for extending his career or, at the very least, not prematurely curtailing it: 'That's the only reason I played so long. I didn't drink because I lived for my sport … sadly, I couldn't say the same about all the players I was with in England.' In an era where footballers' wages are not what they are today, three or four years' extra earning power was not something to be sniffed at.

'Frank was similar to me,' Muhren told Mitten. 'He didn't drink a lot and we shared the same view about the players' drinking, that the players had too much time because they were free from 12 o'clock. That was fine for me because I had a wife and three children, but not for younger players. On several occasions, I was concerned after smelling alcohol at training in the morning. But I realised that I couldn't change the culture on my own, nor could me and Frank change it. You needed the majority of players.'

Amusingly, as we conclude this chapter, Alan Brazil is on record as maybe the most full-throated dissenter from the Muhren-Stapleton-Bailey narrative: 'People talk about drink cultures, but it's there in black and white – look at who ruled Europe [Liverpool] in the 70s and 80s. I know doctors will tell you differently, but what was wrong with our diet then, our booze? I'm adamant it's an absolute load of bollocks that you shouldn't drink.' Let's leave the last word to Stapleton, for whom it's clear cut: 'If Alex Ferguson had been Manchester United manager in the early 80s we would have won the league, probably three times. Not only for the discipline side of it, but he would have put a stop to all the drinking.'

14.

DRINKING TO GET DRUNK

*'Possibly if I had been older, I would have
been more tolerant ... I hope I wouldn't be,
but you never know ...' – Alex Ferguson*

FOR some of United's number, two or three drinks
were *never* enough. In the case of Paul McGrath,
injury was seen as if not the cause of his woes, then
certainly a contributor to his apparent overconsumption.
The defender's time at Old Trafford saw him undergo eight
operations on his busted knee and those were the periods
that he saw as being the worst of his drinking as a player.

McGrath's descent into destructive drinking had started,
albeit inauspiciously, when he was playing for a local side in
Dublin. The team had gone on tour to Germany, and while
there the 18-year-old had sampled some sherry and Pernod.
He was warned by his team-mates 'not to overdo it' but, in
a glimpse as to how his future was to unfold, he blacked
out that night and had to be filled in as to its events. But he
had felt great while he was drinking it: the alcohol bathing

him in a pool of physical and emotional warmth that had previously been lacking.

The young McGrath (or Paul Nwobilo, as he was back then) had grown up in a children's home in Dublin. Essentially an orphanage, it was run by the Protestant Smyly Trust. Though he has some fond memories of that time, it was far from an idyllic childhood. The circumstances which surrounded his residing there, he believes, undoubtedly factored into his emotional state later in life. Moments – not least the separation from his mother – haunted him, leading to him feeling quietly angry and unloved.

He had played well during that trip to Germany, so his drinking appeared to be nothing more than a youthful indiscretion. There was a sense that a move to England was on the horizon and it would likely have come sooner had the young man not had an emotional breakdown, precipitated by his upbringing and the emotional disconnect that it engendered within him. Still, several years later, McGrath was approached by several English clubs. In his mind, though, there was only one destination: Manchester United. He headed over on an initial one-month trial, but before he hopped on the ferry he had celebrated with a bottle of Southern Comfort. It was the first time he had drunk since that time on tour a couple of years earlier.

The boss who had brought him over, Ron Atkinson, was, as we know, famed for his laissez-faire attitude to his players' private business. Yet there was a perception in the wider English game – one that has only grown since – that perhaps it *did* spill over into their footballing capabilities. This was seen especially so in the case of the 'terrible twosome', McGrath and Whiteside, as well as others who were regarded as being part of the Old Trafford dressing room's boozy cabal: Kevin Moran, Gordon McQueen and Bryan Robson.

McGrath and Whiteside's most notable 'on-pitch' booze-related scrapes came on pre- and post-season tours. In the summer of 1985, United were participating in one such tour in the Caribbean, basking in a post-FA Cup-winning glow. Atkinson believed they were about to play a local team and the players were contentedly drinking Carib beer. Alarmingly, it transpired that they were actually facing Southampton, and, when they did, Whiteside had to be taken off after an hour in order that he did not, as Atkinson wrote, 'look[…] a bigger prat than he was already'. On another occasion, McGrath got similarly drunk before a post-season match versus Tottenham. Having consumed a dozen pints, he had played awfully and scuffed a penalty. It led to Atkinson branding him a 'bloody disgrace' and demanding he return early for pre-season.

There were often less constraints for these two Irishmen. Their constant injuries meant they had the opportunity to drink more or less as they pleased. In the 1983/84 season, McGrath featured in just nine matches in all competitions and achieved only 23 appearances the following term. In the early years, lager was the most popular item on his personal menu. Later, it was supplemented by plentiful servings of vodka. Drinking was something to do to pass the time, to ease the boredom. It was not as if he had any other hobbies anyway, and he always had a willing accomplice in Whiteside.

For these two most stubborn members of the dressing-room drinkers' club, there would likely have been little that would have persuaded them to change their ways. As Whiteside acknowledged, 'It was just different in those days. You had a drink and worked it off in the gym the next day. We were injured so the opportunity was always there. We had no game to work up to. It meant you could be out seven nights a week if you wanted to.' Both he and McGrath were seen to be taking liberties, unfocussed on the task of getting back to anything resembling match fitness.

After Alex Ferguson supplanted Atkinson in the Old Trafford hot seat in 1986, he would take a firmer line. At least when he laid in to Whiteside he gave something back, trying to defend himself or explain his whereabouts. 'He was intelligent and would hold his hand up when called to account over his drinking,' Ferguson said. 'At least in our talks I felt I was communicating with Norman.' McGrath, whose drinking was undoubtedly more serious, would wilt, letting the manager's angry words blow past him.

Ferguson's direct approach was not suited to all, especially McGrath, for whom the ranting and raving was reminiscent of his time at the children's home. His behaviour seemed utterly baffling. After one session, he was offered a lift back from proceedings by Whiteside's wife, Julie, but declined and ended up crashing his car into a wall. 'We told no one,' McGrath said. 'I went back to playing football again, being normal, I was like someone who had done something indiscreet at a party. It was a closed book. A family secret.' Steve Bruce was signed to bolster the central-defensive number but McGrath, as Ferguson noted, 'continued to give abstinence a wide berth'.

On another occasion, he had gone on Granada's *Kick-Off* one Thursday night in January 1989. Not expecting to be anywhere near contention for that weekend's playing squad, he and Whiteside were in an obviously inebriated state. But with his hand forced by injuries to others, Ferguson informed McGrath he would be selected. In the end, he had to be talked down from doing so by physio Jim McGregor. Ferguson recalled that 'The whole week, him and Norman had been on the sauce … When they'd leave the training ground, they'd go somewhere and I'd get a phone call. Then they'd go somewhere else. There was a trail leading right back to where they lived.' Though it may have been amusing in hindsight, Ferguson was furious: 'At the time, I was disgusted by their behaviour.' He fined them, only frustrated that the PFA rules restricted him from imposing a greater financial penalty.

Not long after, Ferguson tried to ease McGrath into retirement by offering two years' wages – around £100,000 – to hang up his boots. Whiteside, who he could still get through to, was sent to Lilleshall for a month to get fit. They were both put on the transfer list. At 29, McGrath felt that, tempting as it was, he was too young to jack it in. For both he and Whiteside, it had come after a litany of incidents that had tested the patience of the Scotsman. 'There was one morning,' Ferguson wrote, 'the two of them had been in some bar down in the meat market. A place that opened at four in the morning or something like that. And they came straight in from training. Of course, by the time they came in, somebody's phoned me. You could tell they were pissed, just the smiles on their faces.'

It was generally accepted that McGrath's knees probably only had two or three seasons left in them, though this was not the reasoning behind his eventual departure from Old Trafford. 'In the end,' Ferguson explained, 'him leaving United had nothing to do with his ability. It was to do with how I was going to change Manchester United. And there was a ruthlessness about it. But I had to be ruthless. I felt if I don't make my mark, I'm going to die here.'

Splitting the difficult duo up that August – Whiteside to Everton for £800,000 and McGrath to Aston Villa for half that – seemed a logical step. Ferguson contended that he had tried everything, including calling in a parish priest, Francis McHugh, to minister to the centre-back. It was a claim which McGrath mocks, since he was not a regular in the pews of Manchester's Catholic churches. 'I didn't register with him,' Ferguson said, 'although having a sympathy of a kind for Paul McGrath … I sensed that he was on a self-destruct course.'

His obligation, as manager, was to the club and not its players. 'I had,' Ferguson wrote, 'to get rid of this idea that Manchester United were a drinking club, rather than a football club.' McGrath, of course, did not fit that mould: 'I believe he sought refuge in a lifestyle which, of course, created conflict with my concept of a Manchester United player.' Ferguson needed to make an example of him, to dispel any notion that it would be business as usual. McGrath has since stated that he would have done the same thing in the circumstances: he and Whiteside both needed a fresh start somewhere else.

Before his unveiling at Villa Park, McGrath drank Southern Comfort in Graham Taylor's car to quell his nerves. Here the player had a manager who had learned quickly that he was the sort of person who needed a gentle chat and a supportive nudge rather than being yelled at. After an incident when McGrath had made another attempt on his own life, Taylor had told him, 'Look, son, there are bigger things in life than football.' The centre-back felt comfortable going to see him for a chat and recognised that he had saved him from 'a bad, bad scene'. Taylor is even said to have confided in his wife that he would have been tempted to drink heavily if he had had some of the challenges McGrath had faced in his early years.

For McGrath, there were days when it simply came down to not liking who was staring back at him in the mirror. He had, to his detriment, come to realise that he could drink close to games and still play reasonably well, at least to the extent that he could get away with it. In other moments, he would sneak a drink in the match setting whichever way he could; during winter, the players would be dispensed a small shot of brandy with the intention of keeping them warm. McGrath was blacklisted from receiving this ration, so he would send Shaun Teale – who would not usually partake – to get him one and quietly pass it to him.

There are four games during his career where he describes himself as being 'drunk as a lord' and perhaps another ten where he was certainly more inebriated than would be advisable. Yet that first season with Villa was a good one. He missed just three games as they battled to a second-place finish, and in 1992/93 he was voted PFA Player of the Year.

When McGrath was reunited with Ron Atkinson at Villa Park after Taylor left to manage England, he was allowed to room alone. He had not enjoyed having to share a room and, in any case, could not have been much fun to share with. His team-mates' sidelong glances at his forays into the minibar got in the way of what he wanted – *needed* – to do.

As far as international duty was concerned, the club took extra precautions, often sending someone to Dublin to ensure he got straight home after his duty had been done. Teale, who had reluctantly abetted him in his dressing-room alcohol acquisition, believed that 'Paul [sometimes] drank to get rid of his pain ... I honestly believe that later in his career the pain in his knees was pushing him towards drink.

'Because he knew that football was his lifeblood,' Teale continued, 'once it finished, he could really have a problem, he was terrified of finishing.' All the while he continued plying his trade as a footballer, his arthritis was worsening. Jim Walker, who had played for Derby under Brian Clough and was Villa's physio, essentially became his minder and confidant. He would rescue McGrath from untoward situations he found himself in and even, sometimes, sleep outside McGrath's hotel-room door, as well as lending a listening ear during some of the more trying passages of the player's life. As long as he was playing football, he was just about fine, but ask him to do anything else like speak to some children at a school, Atkinson observed, and he would be terrified.

His team-mates, particularly on international duty, were not always able to grasp the severity of his issues. As Kevin Moran noted, 'Back then, there was never a day I would have thought, "Bloody hell, this guy has a major problem." Everybody was just out ... it was very much founded on lads going out and enjoying themselves. To the extent that it was just amazing how well we did.' It would be unthinkable now and more than likely held United back even then: 'To think that you could go out on a Sunday night till all hours before a game on a Wednesday. And all hours was all hours,' Moran said.

McGrath, unlike most of his team-mates – even when they were consuming a lot – was not drinking to be sociable. He was drinking to get drunk. To an extent, he was protected. The club did not want stories to get out (for his sake and theirs) and it was well before the advent of camera phones and being able to publish through social media. For the battle-worn Irishman, he would rather not be drinking with people he knew at all. It was easier that way. When he reflected on the designation of 'alcoholic' which he had become encumbered in his autobiography, he wrote: 'I'm not sure alcoholism is explainable to people unaffected by it. It is a choice thing. But maybe not in the way that most imagine. When the time comes to drink, there's not much that can draw you back from it.'

After retiring from football, one label which McGrath did not feel comfortable with was that of 'ex-footballer'. At first, retirement was a relief, the pressures associated with the game were gone and it allowed more time with family. But it was scary, too. Alcoholics need to keep busy. Not only had McGrath lost his identity as a footballer, which is tough enough for many, he was an alcoholic, too.

More recently, McGrath's life has been characterised by bouts of sobriety punctuated with tragic, devastating drinking interludes. Living with his first wife, he tried to wean himself off the drink. Unable to shed the deceitfulness that comes with active alcoholism, he was regularly picked up by the police and dropped back to his home, of sorts, with Claire.

After an incident which had led to an arrest, one police officer poignantly informed him that he used to watch him from the Stretford End and hoped he could get well. Eventually McGrath, who had become close friends with Roy Keane, reached a tipping point with his erstwhile wife. He found himself discharged by the court with nowhere to go, wandering around for a day before finding himself on the doorstep of an old friend. This saw him redirected back to the Rutland Centre, and another spell in the Priory. The cycle began again, with the hope that this time it would stick.

It was at Sheffield United, under Nigel Spackman, that he finally had to give up the fight against his own knees. There were some drunk games there, too. McGrath would joke that his breath could have knocked over opposition strikers and that he would 'hold [his] breath in games so they could not smell the drink'. Tranquillisers, in the form of Zimovane, had become a factor too, another way of coping. With the matches gone, now the binge drinking could become an unrestricted affair with any pretence of control abandoned. Pretence, here, is the operative word.

Though he had enjoyed the best of his career at Villa Park, drink had still been an unavoidable elephant in the room. He would encourage the nervous trainee whose car he was travelling in to training at Bodymoor Heath to stop off at an off-licence on the way, buying himself some cans to keep himself topped up.

McGrath did recognise that the game had changed by the time he left it. Speaking to the *Daily Mail*, he admitted 'it was a case of, "Jeez, I'm going to have to be half-right if I want this to continue." People were stepping away from it.' Looking back on how it had been when he had entered the game fresh off the ferry from Dublin, he continued, 'We had the mentality that if you win a game then you would go out. The food was changing, they were bringing in psychologists. Not that it would have done much good with me.' Persisting with that theme, he said, 'They could have locked me in a room with six or seven of them and, no doubt about it, they'd all have left first. I'd have screwed the lot of them up.'

Being anonymous as Paul McGrath in Ireland, where he had returned, was a challenge. He readily admitted in his autobiography that he did not get to enough AA meetings, struggling because he was such a recognisable face at certain venues. When his second marriage broke down in 2003, there was even a spell at the Sporting Chance clinic, although his stay (albeit with his consent) unfortunately featured as part of a BBC documentary on the then new clinic.

Paul Merson was another of the show's 'stars' as he attempted to reckon with renewed gambling problems. The wisdom of this move, ostensibly so that Tony Adams could attract new investment to the venture and reduce his own financial commitment, seems questionable. Both men were vulnerable and their anonymity at the level of 'press, radio and films' ought to have been the top priority. McGrath admitted he was not 'the best advert' for Sporting Chance, given that he ended up in court during its filming. It was, on balance, a situation he shouldn't have been put in.

15.

FERGIE TIME

*'I didn't want people to get the impression
that drinking was part of life with
Manchester United'* – Alex Ferguson

*'To hell with the soft-shoeing around such a
major issue'* – Alex Ferguson

ALEX Ferguson had inherited a wayward dressing room from Ron Atkinson. Even if its extent has been disputed by his predecessor, there was certainly more than a kernel of truth to it. The evidence was there the moment Fergie had taken up the reins: Atkinson had invited many of the team to his boozy leaving do.

That was just 48 hours before the side faced Oxford in a fixture they lost 2-0. Ferguson's ire was drawn by Atkinson's departing act; a party at his house to mark his sacking at which some – mostly injured – players were present. It was supposed to be a small gathering but 'instead it turned into an all-night rave with more than a hundred people packed into the house. It lasted until about five o'clock the following morning.' Atkinson, writing in his autobiography, stressed that 'it was never a case of revenge ... The big-time bunch were all out of contention at the time due to injury.'

In normal circumstances, Big Ron only forbade drinking in the two days before a match, something which his Scottish successor described as 'feeble prohibition'. Under the new regime, if a player was 'in training' he should not be drinking and those who strayed too far beyond the line were shipped out. Ferguson wrote that before he turned up and cracked the whip, United was 'more of a social club than a football club'. Atkinson rubbished those claims in his own account of the era. 'Under me,' he wrote, 'Manchester United were a team that were supposed to have drunk themselves into oblivion ... That was a massive exaggeration. Alcohol was part of the temper of the times in English football and it was not confined to Manchester United.'

When Ferguson arrived, United had not won the title for 19 years and the new boss knew that certain aspects of the dressing-room culture would have to change, telling his players 'I've a difficulty here ... I can't change who I am. So you all need to change who you are!' Frank Stapleton knew the writing was on the wall for a number of the squad: 'I couldn't see that people were going to last long if they continued drinking because Alex wasn't going to tolerate it. And he had the backing of the board to do whatever he wanted.'

Gordon Strachan tells a story in which Alex Ferguson was in a taxi on the way home from a match as manager of Aberdeen. While in transit, he heard another taxi being ordered to Pittodrie to convey four of his players to a nightclub. He ordered his own vehicle to turn around, returning to the stadium to reprimand his players and demand that they go home instead. As it was in Scotland, so it would be in south Lancashire.

Ferguson wanted to put a stop to the drinking entirely. He would permit a glass of wine on a Saturday night, but even this concession displeased the manager. Since then, Bryan Robson has been keen to emphasise that what had gone before was not a scene of unbridled debauchery: 'I don't want anyone running away with the idea that Ron was happy for us to go out boozing every night, far from it,' Robson wrote. Under the new regime, the players were not prepared to cease all consumption but their habits did change. Robson largely confined his drinking to weekends if the team had a match during the week and suggested that he would only drink with his team-mates a couple of times a month during the season. If Monday had witnessed a big session, 'I wouldn't touch another drop for the rest of the week,' he said, keen to refute allegations that drink ever 'took the edge off [his] game'.

Whiteside noted a discernible difference in managerial style post-Atkinson, 'There's no doubt he'd hear stories about us being out and about. But he wouldn't come running around the pubs trying to find us. Fergie would. He'd go from one end of Altrincham to the other, dipping his head into pubs ...' He and McGrath had begun to feel surveilled, as if they were not trusted. Which, broadly speaking, was true. Yet the drinking did not stop entirely, although, in Ferguson's own words, 'I stopped the lunchtime binges and made sure they knew how I felt about that aspect of their lives.' He could not jettison anyone at first, in part because budgetary constraints meant he would not have been able to replace them. The culture could not be altered overnight by the importation of moderating influences, so it would be an attritional process over the next four years.

Despite everything, Ferguson believed that if he had signed Paul Gascoigne – as he very nearly did – that he could have been the one to set him on the right path. He conceded that it would be 'no joyride', but wrote that 'maybe his self-destructive nature would have brought him trouble anywhere, but it is my belief that if he had signed for United he would not have had nearly as many problems as he had in London'.

In some battles, the players would simply ignore Ferguson. On one trip to the Middle East they were told they could have a few drinks in the afternoon. When afternoon turned to evening they chose to carry on regardless, long into the night. For Ferguson, it was a shock.

His time at Aberdeen dealing with younger, lesser-known individuals had not prepared him for this level of subordination from his playing staff. In Scotland he would 'ban' players after discovering them drinking, letting them believe their careers were over until he was satisfied the message had been absorbed.

After discovering that the Waterloo bar was the scene of numerous misdemeanours relating to his St Mirren squad, he ranted at them furiously, smashing a Coke bottle in the dressing room and demanding they sign a collective agreement not to return there. 'Boozing,' he said, 'should have no place in the life of a professional sportsman.' He believed it was a 'blight on the discipline of British footballers'.

Later, he accepted that the commonly held view that he was a hard taskmaster was entirely correct. He had to be. But he also came to concede that his approach had been naive; some of the players required an arm around their shoulder rather than the full hairdryer treatment. Evidence of Ferguson's mentality is corroborated by the recollections of Billy Garton: 'I had a mixed bag with Alex,' he told Mitten in *We're The Famous Man United*. 'I got in trouble a couple of times for coming in late. He wanted people to report players if they were out pissed up, misbehaving. He nurtured a grass mentality which put everyone on guard. I can understand why he did it because a lot of players were going off the rails by drinking in the afternoon.'

Ferguson's routine saw him arrive at the training ground at 7.30 each morning. Training began at 10.30am as it had been under Atkinson, but now players were required to report to the Cliff by 9.30. There had been times when Big Ron himself had arrived late to training. That would certainly not be happening under the new incumbent. Porridge and vegetables became training-ground staples at the Cliff as Ferguson's new broom swept through. He terrified several players, not least Peter Barnes, who hid while Fergie administered hairdryer treatments to the squad and later criticised him in the press. Colin Gibson, a left-back who was sold to Leicester, said Ferguson nearly drove him to drink.

Some of their manager's anger, it is argued, was an affectation, a deliberate technique to flush out those who did not have the *cojones* to compete at the level he believed the club should aspire to. Bryan Robson has suggested that, 'He did that to find out their character. He would see how a player responded. If a player wilted, then he would have got rid of them because he would have felt that their character wasn't strong enough to play at United.' Robson was one of the few who avoided the full heat of Ferguson's fiery breath: 'I never got the hairdryer,' he said. 'But I saw people who did. I was close to them at the time. And I was happy to remain goody two shoes.'

Robson, much like Adams and Merson would later become at Arsenal, was a classic 'son of' the manager. Though a renowned drinker, he was a professional too. At least, more so than Whiteside or McGrath were deemed to be. Like them, he was a regular on the treatment table and Ferguson made clear that recovering from injury would not be aided by time in the pub. 'Drinking is unacceptable at any time,' he wrote, 'but in spells of enforced idleness it is even more of a menace and certain to slow down the process of rehabilitation.' Robson was able to sweat it out when he was fully fit but, Ferguson said, 'Bryan's unwillingness to give up booze altogether caused our relationship to be fraught now and again.'

The proof was in the pudding. Second bottom of the league when Ferguson showed up, United finished 11th that season.

Ferguson's attitude to alcohol, it should be said, was not one stemming from austere religiosity. After he had retired from his playing career at Rangers, he had even run a pub at the junction of Glasgow's Govan and Paisley

Roads, frequented by dockers working on the banks of the Clyde. 'Pubs,' he wrote, 'taught me about people, their dreams and frustrations, in a way that complemented my efforts to understand the football trade.' He had spent the last 18 months of his playing career helping in a friend's pub, and when it ended he was offered one of his own by the Drybrough brewery. It was renamed 'Fergie's' and, along with a second venue acquired with a loan from the same Edinburgh brewery, remained under his supervision until he became Aberdeen manager.

In his years as a manager, he was known for the bottle of Claret he kept in his office for the visit of an opposition's manager after a game. More than anything else, it was the *type* of drinking that was going on that troubled him. 'I don't mind drink in celebration of a great result,' he wrote, 'but it had become woven into the fabric of United.'

Famously, Ferguson resorted to visiting players in their houses when he suspected something was amiss. He once got wind of a supposed party at Lee Sharpe's house. 'I opened Sharpey's door,' Ryan Giggs told *The Telegraph*. 'I was holding a [bottle of] Beck's and there was no escape.' It was not, Sharpe has since clarified, a 'full-scale party', as Ferguson had described it. The bottles of Beck's in question were the last ones left in the house, he said, and the players – including three apprentices, to whom Ferguson administered a clip round the ear as they left – were actually getting ready for a night out on the town. Ferguson's informant, it has since transpired, was Giggs's own mother. Sharpe told *The Independent*, 'It was just bad timing, that's all.' Nevertheless, he said, it was a story that 'went a long way towards fuelling all those myths about my lifestyle'.

Though the methods were draconian, Ferguson's players look back on that period in a different light. 'I appreciate it now,' Giggs told the newspaper, 'but at the time, it was a pain. You'd go out on a Saturday night and he'd tell you where you were, what you'd done and who you were with. You'd think: "How does he know that?" He just knew everyone. If I came here for training clean shaven, he'd say I'd been out the night before.' Such was the control Ferguson exercised over Giggs's career that he was not permitted to do any interviews until the age of 20 and only acquired an agent when his manager eventually consented.

Sharpe, who had once dared to call his manager Alex rather than 'gaffer' or 'boss', recalled a tete-a-tete with Ferguson in the early 90s, during which Ferguson wondered, rhetorically, why the players insisted on going out after Wednesday night games. Surely, he proffered, if they were going to have a few drinks, it would be better to do it at home. Giggs, Sharpe, Roy Keane and Gary Pallister, the players on the receiving end, asked him, 'What's the difference if we're sat at home or in a bar, boss?' In their eyes, it was harmless. 'We just go out, have a few beers, a bit of a chat, and that's it.'

Eventually, Sharpe said, Ferguson had to 'agree to disagree' about their apparent need to sink a few pints to unwind. In any case, one of their number, Pallister, was – according to Clayton Blackmore – a 'lightweight' who drank Malibu and Coke, something Blackmore deemed a 'woman's drink'. After one session, Pallister had gone outside for some fresh air and promptly collapsed. 'I thought he was dead,' Blackmore said. Blackmore, who was the only surviving member of the team from Ferguson's first fixture against Oxford by the time 1990 rolled around, recalled, 'I could drink, but Robbo was the benchmark. Robbo used to drink more than us and still train by himself on his day off to run off the drink.' In 1991, a teetotaller arrived in the form of Andrei Kanchelskis.

The manager's hard-line stance may have seemed somewhat restrictive at the time, but, with the benefit of hindsight, it seems Sharpe's star would have shone brighter if only he had remained under the Scotsman's watchful eye. 'With young players you have to try to impart a sense of responsibility. If they can add greater awareness to their energy and their talents they can be rewarded with great careers,' Ferguson wrote in his second autobiography with Giggs and Sharpe in mind. 'I am keen,' he explained, 'to educate [young players] about the dangers they encounter as their careers progress, especially about how damaging a freewheeling attitude to drink can be.'

Although Sharpe claimed Ferguson 'victimised' him and 'ruined his career', the winger had made his debut for United at 17, played for England at 19 and became the PFA Young Player of the Year that same season. Yet he lost his way, sold to Leeds United for £4.5 million in 1996 by his strictest of disciplinarians. By 28, he was playing for Bradford City which, as charitably as possible, is not where he should have been given the potential he had displayed. The last of his eight England caps came in 1993, when Sharpe was just 22. By 31, he was without a club.

At one stage, when he was 20, Ferguson had even ordered him to leave his own house and return to his digs, believing that a spate of poor performances were related to distractions beyond the pitch. He had, Ferguson believed, granted him independence when he was too young to shoulder it and informed the player, 'Sharpie, to make it to the top in football you need to sacrifice.' More recently, Sharpe told *FourFourTwo*, 'He scared me to death, pretty much ... Probably Liverpool was the worst [time] when he kicked me out of my house. The girlfriend had moved up from Birmingham, she had to go back home and we split up. My dog had to get sold, my car had to get sold and I had to go out there and prove to him I could play.'

As this section draws to a close, we might be amused to find out that Ferguson saw a technological solution to resolve any future infractions: 'I believe that some day soon we will be able to test them each morning and if they have been drinking they will simply be sent home.' Just as long as that home was approved by Sir Alex, of course.

IV
THE RECOVERY

16.

HEARTS OF GOLD, FEET OF CLAY

A T the height of Paul Merson's drinking, he was going out five nights a week. The daily cycle involved jumping in a taxi to training, struggling through the morning, before having some lunch and then getting back on it again.

Rinse, and repeat. There were arrests, such as the time he became involved in a pub fight where a pool cue was brandished as a weapon. Then there was a prosecution for drink-driving aged just 18, after a botched attempt to drive home from the Rose and Crown in St Albans. Clipping almost every car in his path, he knocked over a lamppost. This earned him an 18-month driving ban and a £350 fine. After that, he had moved in with his girlfriend Lorraine, to a house which sat conveniently between two pubs.

As a young teenager, Merson would drink to calm the panic attacks, which would occasionally paralyse him. It was just a few Pernod and blacks with his schoolboy friends. Sometimes, he would drink at home too, on Saturday nights when his mum and dad had gone out for a meal with friends. They would return to find him passed out on the sofa surrounded by cans.

A few short years later, Merson was coming through the ranks at Arsenal and could count Charlie Nicholas and Graham Rix as drinking buddies. With, as we're well aware by now, a day off most Wednesdays, Arsenal players could get extravagantly drunk on Tuesdays. Most of them did: Merson, Steve Bould, Tony Adams, Nigel Winterburn and Perry Groves were all among the Tuesday club luminaries. Later their numbers were supplemented by the attendance of Ray Parlour and, sometimes, Alan Smith. By this time, our protagonist could comfortably put away 15 pints in a session.

His manager, George Graham, seemed relaxed about the situation as long as the squad were fine by Thursday. According to Merson, Perry Groves arrived as a 'teetotaller' and left the club in 1992 a 'serious drinker'. When John Jensen had been signed that same year, he brought with him the nickname 'Faxe', a hat tip to a brand of Danish beer that had contributed to Jensen's reputation as a renowned boozer at Brøndby. Any reputation he had there, however, soon paled into insignificance by Arsenal's standards.

'My problem came from the fact that I used booze to put my head right,' Merson recalled. When he was a Youth Training Scheme scholar in his early days at the club, drinking would help quieten the nerves of the shy young man, who used to get palpitations during schoolboy matches. By the time he was a first teamer, he drank alcohol to help maintain the high that the buzz of scoring and winning brought.

There was quite a lot of winning, too: league titles in 1989 and 1991, an FA and League Cup double in 1993, as well as a European Cup Winners' Cup the following year. In 1989 he was even recognised as the PFA Young Player of the Year. To an extent, he was getting away with it, at least in a footballing context. Concealing the booze-related weight gain from physios was easier in an age before the fitness department was aided by sophisticated technology. Merson would simply lean to one side while he was on the scales, calling out a lower number than the one showing on the dial.

In a pre-social media era, rival fans would send letters to the club reporting that they had seen Merson out of his tree in various locations. Often, their contents were true, but one verifiably fake report – the whole team had been overseas at the time – gave Merson the excuse that they must *all* be from mischievous Tottenham fans. Sometimes, when George Graham discovered one of Merson's indiscretions, the player would be dropped and told to go away for a couple of weeks to sort himself out. Inevitably, Merson saw this as another opportunity to drink more. On another occasion, Graham named him as a sub to teach him a lesson when he was hungover. Merson fell asleep on the bench, so Graham brought him on for the last ten minutes of a match Arsenal won 4-1.

Terry Venables – who had become England manager at the start of 1994 – fielded Merson in a friendly against Greece at Wembley in May 1994. The home nation won 5-0, but their number eight did not perform well and Venables never picked him again. It continued the trajectory that had begun under Graham Taylor, who was once overheard by several parties saying, 'Merson, now he's a good player. Only trouble is you don't know what will happen next, whether he'll be carried out of a taxi legless. Put a pint of lager in the middle of the goal and he'll get it.'

The problem was that one was never enough. When an abstemious team-mate asked him if he wanted to go out for a single pint, Merson could not understand. 'One? What's the point in that?' The reality was that for Merson, as an alcoholic, one is too many but, as the saying in Alcoholics Anonymous goes, 100 is never enough. As he wrote himself, 'Everything I ever did was all or nothing: football, gambling and drinking.' This concurred with memories of conversations he had with David Seaman, during which he had told the goalkeeper, 'If I cannot get drunk, I wouldn't even bother having a drink … he used to think I was always messing around.'

In the long term, the drinking proved to be unmanageable. Regular 14-pint sessions had rendered Merson a stone and a half overweight. Funded by his £5,000 a week wage, his intake had taken a toll on his ability to train, particularly as Graham's sessions were known for being physically demanding. Merson had been holding it together – just – for some time but his life was beginning to fall apart.

The gambling, which had started with his first pay cheque from Arsenal when he was 16, was out of control. He was ploughing ever larger sums through his bookmaker's accounts and, in doing so, widening the fractures in his marriage to Lorraine. On 3 November 1994, after a poor performance in a Cup Winners' Cup match against

Brøndby, Merson knew the charade was over. A few years later, he acknowledged to *The Independent*, 'Not scoring, but us going through, probably [did me] a favour. If I'd have scored everything would have been all right that night.' Though it would not become public knowledge until weeks later, that was the night that Paul Merson had reached his own jumping-off point.

At the time, Tony Adams – still drinking heavily – saw his friend as weak, someone who had never been in his league as a drinker, capitulating in the face of a few pints. George Graham, 'a very understanding man', gave his wayward winger a week off to sort things out and re-establish his fitness. Not all of their team-mates were fully cognisant of the internal battles that were raging inside of their alcoholic team-mates' heads. Alan Smith said of Merson, 'I used to get changed next to Paul before every game. I got asked so many times about whether I guessed there were real problems, but, honestly, I didn't. Nowadays, there are much firmer tabs kept on players – but not so much back then.' Perry Groves is well aware that it was a different time: 'If modern Arsenal players sank as many beers as we did, they'd struggle to stay in the division. We were athletes, but these guys are pyrotechnic. They look different. The change is incredible.'

The secrets and lies were all part of Merson's tortured mental state and he needed the whispers to stop. After training on 24 November, Merson headed to the offices of the *Daily Mirror* to tell Harry Harris his story. The headline the next day read 'Don't kick me out of football', with Merson pleading in the paragraphs that followed, 'I haven't brought the game into disrepute – I've brought myself into disrepute.' Behind the scenes, Arsenal and the FA were negotiating what the next step should be. Alcohol and gambling were one thing – not inherently illegal – but the cocaine use was quite another and some plan of action would be expected. After all, Merson was the first player still active in the game to admit to drug taking.

The player had escaped the country hours after speaking to Harris, and when the wave of headlines cascaded down in the early hours of the following morning he and Lorraine were already in France. This was important, not least because there were certain revelations about which Lorraine was not fully aware. Merson would tell her while they were away in order that her first encounter with some of the more lurid details was on his terms. What was supposed to have been a week on the continent became a truncated visit. Arsenal and the FA needed him to return, to face the music and take the punishment they were about to dole out to him.

It was at an emotional press conference on 29 November that Merson faced his accusers in the tabloid press. The FA's Graham Kelly had already informed him that he would not play again until he had gone to rehab and completed a course of treatment. They had decided on a strategy of brutal frankness both with Merson – who was told he would need to treat rehab seriously – and with the press, who would be spared no detail of his situation. A joint statement between the club and the association was issued, which explained that the player would be resident at a treatment facility for at least six weeks, a spell funded by the payment Merson had received for *The Mirror*'s exclusive. Before announcing it all to the waiting media, Merson had already attended his first Gamblers Anonymous meeting.

Arsenal chairman Peter Hill-Wood was firm in his assessment of the circumstances, but understanding too. 'The boy is in a mess,' he wrote. 'His career is in disarray. But Arsenal are not going to throw the book at him. Merson has gone beyond that type of punishment.' Describing the player as not having 'a particularly high intelligence', he believed that 'somewhere inside Paul is a smashing boy [who is] unable to cope with the fame and fortune football has brought him'. Finding it hard to reconcile the Merson on the pitch with the timid boy from Essex off it, Hill-Wood concluded, 'I have never known somebody with such expression as a footballer yet lacking such self-confidence as a person.' Despite all of this, he declared 'not once has it been discussed to kick him out of the club. That is not Arsenal's way.'

Merson had described football as a release, yet the buzz of scoring a goal – even if it was the best feeling in the world – was short, and drinking 'kept [his] high up'. Had he been drinking to blot out a failing career or a serious injury that might have provided an explanation, if not an excuse. Yet he was doing well, winning things with Arsenal. There seemed to be no simple explanation for what had planted this destructive seed inside him. The fact was that his problems were there, irrespective of their cause, and what was important was what he was going to do about them.

The Saturday after Merson had laid bare his soul, Arsenal fans began singing, 'There's only one Paul Merson' at 3.18pm. It was a demonstration of the large well of goodwill that existed for him. By now he was in the Marchwood Priory hospital, though it had not been easy. He had wanted a guarantee that he would be able to go home for Christmas, but when this was not given he had threatened to leave. His counsellor, Stephen Stephens, told him that he could not put conditions on his treatment programme and, eventually, Merson relented. As it transpired, because Merson completed his step four (known as the most daunting of AA's 12 steps due to its requirement for brutal honesty) before Christmas, he was allowed to spend the day with his family in St Albans, returning to Marchwood on Boxing Day.

Stephens went on to be a key figure in Merson's time at Marchwood and a continuing influence in his life. He wrote in the foreword to Merson's first autobiography, *Rock Bottom*, that 'when someone with an addiction is ill their medicine is other people'. With this in mind, Merson became a frequent attendee at meetings of Alcoholics Anonymous and Gamblers Anonymous, as well as Narcotics Anonymous.

In the rooms of AA and the halls of Marchwood, he was just another alcoholic or another gambler. 'When I got to Marchwood Priory hospital,' he said, 'I no longer felt like a soccer star.' When he eventually left treatment on 13 January 1995, he was given just an hour to pack, ready to be released into the wild again. A further press conference was arranged to announce his progress, at which he broke down in tears – of pain, but also of joy. When he could no longer speak for himself, George Graham held his leg under the table and questions were directed towards the experts beside him.

AC Milan were Arsenal's opponents in the first fixture after Merson had been discharged from the Priory. Stephens was dispatched to spend some time with him before kick-off, even if it was limited to a ten-minute pep-talk in Highbury's home dressing room due to his getting stuck in traffic. Among the substitutes that night, when Merson took to the field for the final 16 minutes of the game in front of 38,000 fans, he did so 10lb lighter than he had been when he had played against Brøndby. The crowd had been calling for him to come on with cries of 'Merson, Merson' and shouts of 'Bring on Merson', and he received applause from the whole ground at the final whistle as a picture of him beside the word 'HOPE' appeared on the scoreboard.

Before his first away game post-release, against Sheffield Wednesday, the club allowed him to absent himself on the Friday evening to go to a 12-step meeting in the steel city, dressed in his club tracksuit. George Graham had, perhaps understandably, wondered if he would be going off for a drink instead. Merson knew he would have to work to earn the trust of the people he had been letting down for years.

The Cup Winners' Cup semi-final versus Genoa saw another Arsenal victory over Italian opposition, despite a missed Merson penalty. As the champagne flowed Merson had to be careful, choosing to sit with Ian Wright on the plane back to London. Wright, as in his dealings with Adams, seems to have had an understanding of his team-mates' issues and adapted his own behaviour accordingly, opting for an orange juice in solidarity. Steve Bould, by contrast, would misguidedly offer Merson an alcopop, believing that it would be permissible because it was 'fruit-based'.

When he had a bad game, Merson could no longer drink to blot it out. Likewise, when a match had gone well he would not be able to sustain the high with a drink or 15. Sometimes this involved separating himself from the drinkers, as he had done on the flight back from Italy. Gary Lewin was a teetotaller and therefore a good candidate as a solid travelling companion. Quite apart from anything else, the strong threat of disciplinary action from the FA loomed over Merson if he slipped back into the powdery aspect of his addiction.

Inside the rooms of Alcoholics Anonymous, Merson was finally among people he could open up to – 'there was nobody in the team I could really confide in' – trusting them enough that he quickly went from telling them nothing to extreme honesty, because he knew that was what he needed to do to stay sober. When it came time for him to do his first 'chair', which involved sharing his own story before other members gave feedback with their own experience, it lasted 45 minutes. It is a distinction he shares with this author. Typically, a chair should last for no more than 20 minutes but that first one is rarely compliant.

Two weeks after Merson had emerged from the Marchwood Priory, George Graham was sacked by Arsenal after being accused of receiving a bung totalling £400,000 in relation to the transfers of John Jensen and Pal Lydersen. It was a blow to Merson, who needed stability as he began to remake his life. Stewart Houston took over until the end of the season but could not command the respect Graham had, and Arsenal ultimately lost the Cup Winners' Cup Final.

It was an early case of Merson having to accept the things he could not change. Similarly, he was told he would have to go on the post-season tour the club had arranged in Hong Kong. He had hoped some consideration would be made of his fragile sobriety, but it was a contractual obligation he would have to meet. Efforts were made to get Stephens along on the trip, but they ultimately proved unsuccessful when he could not secure a visa in time. Nevertheless, arrangements were made for him to attend 12-step meetings while in the city-state.

When asked, as 1996 drew to a close, if he had any New Year's resolutions, Merson joked with a reporter, 'No mate, I've given everything up.' Some of their fellow players believed he and Adams to have become 'recovery bores', devotees of AA who were unable to let loose and enjoy life around them. Though there may be a kernel of truth at times, another team-mate perceptively noted, 'I think it was hard for Paul and Tony's team-mates to really understand what was happening.'

During the 1996/97 season, Merson was an ever-present member of the Arsenal side, signing a new contract which included a clause stating that should he fall off the wagon the agreement would be torn up. It was a detail which was included at his own behest. He had foregone his number ten shirt following the arrival of Dennis Bergkamp at Highbury under Bruce Rioch's direction, reacting in a fairly sanguine fashion to his being usurped. Even so, he believed he could be paid even more somewhere else rather than austere

Arsenal, and when Middlesbrough began sniffing around, he was willing to drop down a division in order to make more money.

It may have been financially wise, but on a personal level it was a move fraught with difficulties. His wife, Lorraine, was understandably loath to displace the entire family to the North East. Merson, not wanting to be isolated from his wife and kids, would drive or get the train from near St Albans up to training early each morning. This too soon proved to be problematic, aggravating injuries and indicating a less than full commitment to the cause of the club that were paying his substantial wages. Eventually, it was decided that he would decamp to a residence closer to Middlesbrough but Lorraine and the boys would stay put in St Albans. As a concession, Merson's brother, Keith, was given a job by the club in order that they could live together and help the footballer keep his nose clean.

This seemed like a reasonable compromise, yet it was one which did not account for Paul Gascoigne being thrown into the mix. In March 1998 Middlesbrough had paid £3.45 million for the midfielder to aid their quest for promotion from the First Division back into the Premiership. The move had benefits for Gascoigne, too; he was performing badly at Rangers and some critics suggested that he needed to be playing in England – even at a second-tier club – in order to realistically compete for a place in the World Cup squad that he would eventually, fatefully, be excluded from. Given that he had arrived towards the end of the season, he was invited to live in Casa Merson which, with the benefit of hindsight, seems like a recipe for disaster and surely cannot have appeared to be a much better idea at the time.

After several years without a drink, a bet or a drug, temptation was staring Merson in the face and his defences were down. One morning he had chosen to commute up from St Albans after a family engagement the previous day. Gascoigne got a train down in order to meet him halfway to keep him company on the rest of his journey. It sounds endearing enough until you realise that Gascoigne was drinking a bottle of wine on the 7.47. Presciently, Merson warned him 'not when we're training and playing. You won't get to the World Cup.' His own situation, as it pertained to a place in the England squad, was looking much brighter: Glenn Hoddle was now in the hot seat and had recalled Merson after a dramatic improvement in form, being responsible for setting up around three-quarters of Middlesbrough's goals.

Here he was, achieving the goal he had set himself when he had left the Marchwood clinic in January 1995: returning to the England fold. Not that it had all been plain sailing. He had gambled again before Gascoigne's entrance on to the scene, and when the Geordie arrived he was on shaky ground. The latter was now using sleeping pills in order to control his daily routine, often taking them as soon as training finished to knock him out for the rest of the day so that he would not eat, drink or otherwise get into mischief. Those pills soon became part of a drinking game involving Merson and Jimmy 'Five Bellies' Gardiner, involving the purchase of apparently expensive wines by Gardiner which they would use to down handfuls of pills.

Each had placed piles of cash on the table and the 'winner' was whoever could stay awake the longest and scoop up their prize. It was Merson's first drink in three and a half years and, although a few wild nights came in its wake, he quickly propelled himself back into the rooms of Alcoholics Anonymous.

'The game isn't over until the final whistle blows,' Merson wrote in *Rock Bottom*. It's a tough lesson to learn, another one that this author shares with the footballer. Staying sober is hard. Staying sober for a long time is even harder. As Merson astutely observes, when alcoholics stop drinking that is not the end of their troubles. Even if they have no craving for the stuff anymore, the alcoholic drink is merely one of the symptoms of their disorder, the warm, soapy balm that they try to apply as a salve to their chaotic mind. If you leave this mental meadow untended for too long, then the old solutions loom into view again.

Since that first relapse, there have been several more. While sad, that is not uncommon. It's just a fact of living with addiction. After a move to Aston Villa came another misstep for Merson. His departure from Middlesbrough had occurred, in part, because of those feelings of unrest after the travails of France 98 had passed. Merson had begun the season with a sense of impending dread, a hunch that something was about to go badly wrong. He had not been going to meetings nor had he made support networks in Middlesbrough. So when the proverbial excrement hit the air filtration device, he was not equipped to deal with the emotions it churned up. Adams, on the other hand, had done things the 'right' way by immersing himself in

Alcoholics Anonymous. When it came time for him to utilise its tenets, the process came naturally.

Early in the 1998/99 season, Merson's finger was poised over what, in AA parlance, is known as the 'fuck it' button. Short on practice with the reflexes that could help him out of a tough spot, he did try to phone his agent, Steve Kutner, to arrange a return to rehab. But when he was unable to get hold of him, his finger finally pressed the dreaded button. He met with Gascoigne, Waddle and Keith Gillespie's agent on a golf course, and when they offered him some Metz (a type of Schnapps) he was powerless to stop himself. A trip to the pub followed, including a game which involved placing a 20-pound note on a dart board with each contestant trying to put three darts through it from various distances.

It was not long before he confessed to Bryan Robson that he needed to go back into treatment but the Middlesbrough boss told him to wait. The manager wondered how serious it was anyway. Perhaps it was just a one-off. These were not the words that Merson needed to hear. Once he had made that declaration, he should have been carted straight off to rehab without a second thought. Yet Robson did not really regard Middlesbrough as a drinking club and thought his player could weather the storm on his own. Gascoigne, Merson thought, was 'probably happy he's found a drinking partner again'. By 10 August, Merson was in Robson's office once more, telling him he thought the best option was to go public about his recent lapses. The manager advised against this, however, and Merson did consider that he might be right, given AA's own urging towards 'restraint of tongue and pen'.

Bryan Robson appeared ill-equipped to deal with one of his star players. Writing in his own autobiography, he admitted, 'When I signed him, I thought he had overcome his demons, but then I had no idea his drink, drugs and gambling problems were as serious as they were.' He did, he said, '[try] to help him and spoke to him about his troubles', but claimed that Merson's attitude could – on bad days – be lacking during training sessions, evident in his body language.

Robson, as we know, had been known as a legendary drinker during his time at Manchester United. The press attention was, he thought, another way to resurrect stories about his own drinking days. 'The press made a big thing of it and, of course, it was a way for them to get at me again,' he said. Robson felt that innocent parties were tarnished by Merson's assertions, too: 'I was annoyed for the other players … [who] went about their work, day in, day out, without giving their manager a moment's bother.' He described it as a 'terrible slur' on those players, suggesting that Merson was trying to 'blame other people for his own, self-inflicted problems'.

Those seem harsh words in the circumstances, betraying an apparent lack of understanding of the battles Merson was trying to fight. *Self-inflicted*. Really? Even so, he had come to expect such coverage around teams he was involved with. In *Robbo*, he wrote, 'Certain sections of the press are always going to look for a chance to churn out the same old rubbish and knock me.'

A few weeks later, Merson had made it clear that he wanted to leave Middlesbrough because of what he saw as a drinking culture at the club. This was something that Gascoigne later thought was a pointed dig at him and which he would deny, saying that he had in fact hidden alcohol when the two lived together. Merson, in turn, would go on to deny this was a reference to his former housemate.

He got his move to Villa but, as he would later discover, this would not solve his problems. It was, he would soon realise, another 'geographical'. Getting perspective on situations is good, but what alcoholics like Merson, Gascoigne, Adams and countless others often forget – wilfully or otherwise – is that we take ourselves with us. When we arrive at that new place – that different town, that different flat – we tend to gravitate towards the same type of friends once again; the people who drink like us, perhaps the people that drink even *more* than we do – or more *recklessly* – in order that we can contextualise the way we carry on as being relatively normal. Alcoholics are skilful at manipulating circumstances, sometimes very subtly, so that they fulfil what they need from them.

Merson's 175-mile move south down the A1(M) was one of these. By 1999 Villa's season had begun to slide precipitously after a phenomenal first few months and Merson's headspace was following a similar trajectory. When they became aware of what was occurring, there were offers of help from fellow England internationals. Teddy Sheringham caught Merson drinking one night in London and tried to persuade him not to consume any more that night, offering to drive him home. Merson told himself that he would just do this once a week, on a Saturday, and though that was a limited success, he could not stop thinking about when the next session would be, who would be there, what he would drink and every single thing that goes along with a night out.

On another occasion, Gareth Southgate had said Merson could stay with him and his wife when Merson was in the area, now that the latter was without a base in Hertfordshire. Southgate had spent a lot of time with Merson and Adams at the World Cup and was among a number of fellow professionals who offered support. Shane Nicholson (of, among others, West Brom and Chesterfield) had found recovery himself and wrote an encouraging letter to Merson around this time. Others had been less helpful: Andy Townsend phoned with Gascoigne in the background urging him to, 'Come and live with me, you bore.'

Ultimately, what Merson needed was to reconnect with people who understood *precisely* where he was coming from. He rang someone from AA and resolved that he would go back into treatment. Informing Villa boss John Gregory of his intention, the manager joked that he had played so well that day he ought to have a drink every Saturday night. It was meant in jest, but Merson was not amused. He was told, in all seriousness this time, that he would need him the following week for a match against Liverpool. Merson could only tell him that he would see how things went. The far more important conversation Merson would have was with Stephen Stephens, calling this process 'getting honest again'.

The importance of narrative to recovering alcoholics should not be underestimated – the ability to foster belonging through confession and sharing. The act of speaking words out loud – willing a new identity into existence – helps that building process. Identity transformation, changing aspects of a personality that need to be discarded in order to survive, is often done through metaphor and storytelling and the vulnerability that comes with disclosure of painful or difficult memories.

Back in the swing of things, he had a new resolve and was 'getting a buzz from [his] football again'. Throughout this period, Adams phoned to encourage him to get along to more AA meetings and it seemed to have the desired effect. Merson wrote of his team-mate, who had a different drinking style than his own – 'I think he was on the piss more than I'd ever been' – and believed that Adams must have looked at Merson and thought, 'well, if he's an alcoholic, then I am.'

In his diaries of this time, Merson wrote 'It's just doing the basics of a recovery programme really, like with football when you're coming back after a bad patch. You practise five-yard passes and it looks easy but how many times in a game do you see players mess them up?' There was some concern for anonymity, but it was outweighed by his desperation to remain sober: 'Meetings are anonymous and I do have trust that no one will say anything outside of the meetings about me. It's people in bars who are likely to go to the papers ... sometimes ... I am worried about what I say because some people know who I am. It is my problem and me who is uncomfortable.'

17.

KEEPING IT SIMPLE

THE stories of the footballers discussed so far in this book have been enlightening, but I wanted to speak to one myself. After several emails and text messages back and forth, I connected with Alan Knight, who made 801 appearances in goal for Portsmouth between 1978 and 2000. 'Like most kids in London,' he told me, 'I always dreamt of being a professional footballer. I was just playing for school teams, Sunday teams and got scouted. I ended up with trials for QPR and Fulham on Wednesday and Thursday nights respectively.'

He was 13 years old then and, while a trialist at Fulham, a scout named Reg Lock took him to Portsmouth. He arrived there at 14 and, two years later, signed apprentice forms. 'I hadn't really had a drink or smoked at that stage,' he explained. 'I was sharing digs with two or three other apprentices; we would go up to the local pub, just drinking orange and water, playing the pinball machine.

'On a Thursday we would get paid in cash,' he said, describing how he 'would have a couple of pints of lager top.' Not long after that, he moved into a guest house which he shared with some of his Portsmouth team-mates. 'I'd half broken into the first team after I made my debut at 16 and I was on the periphery of the first team from 17, so I signed pro at 17 and I was earning a bit more money than the other apprentices who I was with.' He had broken into the squad in 1978, setting him up for a 25-year playing career. This step up meant he went from earning £16 to £60 a week. It was a good wage for the era, and meant he had a disposable income for the first time.

'The guest house was where I got introduced into the drink culture,' he continued. Because he was the reserve goalkeeper in a time before a substitute stopper was included in the matchday squad, 'we'd have the afternoon off, so I'd go with the senior players who were out of the side and we'd end up going to the pub on a Friday afternoon: we weren't travelling and we weren't involved, so I was the young kid following these guys. I'm not blaming them,' he clarified, 'but that's the way it was.'

There were Saturday nights out with the whole team, then Sunday dinner times would be spent at The Cambridge, a pub where they would be entertained by go-go dancers. 'Once I broke into the team it was a case of – especially in the days of Bally [Alan Ball] – that squad that we had then were very close knit; it was all about "you worked hard, you played hard", and we certainly did. We would all work for each other on the pitch and then we would all go out and drink together off the pitch. It was all part of the drink culture and team spirit. I don't think that was any different at Portsmouth than any other club. It built and grew on from there.'

Sunday and Wednesday nights were when the team ventured to the Bird in Hand in the nearby village of Lovedean or the Cowplain Social Club in Waterlooville. After training on Monday, Tuesday and Wednesday, it would be to the Sportsman's Rest – a couple of miles from Fratton Park – for regular sessions which were only curtailed by its 3pm closing time. There were crates of beer on the coach home from away games, quenching the thirst of those players who had observed the 48-hour rule of no drinking before games.

That rule would, of course, be cast aside in favour of greater stricture towards the end of his career. Knight's tenure at the club – first as a player, then as a coach and now in an ambassadorial role – meant he witnessed the changes that rippled through the game, brought about by an injection of television money and greater freedom of contract for players. 'The biggest change at Portsmouth was when more foreign players came into the game and none more so than when Harry Redknapp came in and took over,' Knight said, by now a coach at the club. In February 2004, a year before Redknapp arrived at Portsmouth, they had been the first team to field an XI with each player representing a different nationality. 'I believe Harry made a big difference at Portsmouth Football Club,' Knight continued, 'as he had at West Ham with the decision there to shut the players' bar or have no alcohol in the bar. I still think the English players, the British players, struggled with it for a little while, but I think they began to realise with the changing of contracts that basically they weren't "at it" in themselves and their bodies. Their bodies are their livelihood and they realised that they had to look after themselves, they got more information about how to look after themselves, the sports science side of things.

'Things were happening prior to Harry, but the biggest thing was his arrival and the influx of foreign players because I think the British players then saw more of the culture of what goes on abroad and I think they understood it a little bit better.'

Knight regards the advent of social media as another cause of behavioural change. If players *are* drinking, they cannot be seen to be doing it. Instead, they must be 'doubly careful', he said. 'Obviously there are disadvantages to modern-day social media that players have to be aware of. I think we would have struggled if that was about in our day!'

There were different pressures back then. 'If you didn't come drinking, you weren't one of the lads. Don't get me wrong, I didn't go kicking and screaming, but there were some lads who didn't want to do that and if you took that stance then you had to be strong-willed and be some sort of player for that to be accepted. If you weren't, then you were going to struggle and that was wrong, but that was the macho image of the footballer back in that time, that's the way it was and you couldn't question it, you couldn't show any sort of weakness.' There were, he believed, players who struggled with their mental health, but it would have been inconceivable that they could be open about it 'because it would have been a sign of weakness and you couldn't show any sign of weakness'.

'There was no support network then,' he explained, 'and I think a lot more still needs to be done. There's a lot of professionals and stuff that goes on and when it's the flavour of the month people are all over it but then it's pushed to the back and forgotten. I think it was Danny Rose who said something about how he wouldn't want his kid being a professional footballer and telling parents to have a good think about it, and I would agree with that. Unless they're going to a club they really know, they have to keep an eye on their child because there are so many things that happen later on, so I get what he was saying. But people say "oh well you're a footballer, you've got an easy life, you've got millions of pounds", but that's not the case across all football. Some obviously earn big dough, but some don't and sometimes the transition from being a footballer into the real world is difficult. Some can do it, some can't, there's lots and lots of pitfalls.'

It was the PFA who helped signpost Knight to the right help, some years after he had read Tony Adams's *Addicted*. Back then, he didn't think he was an alcoholic but had a sense that *something* was up and understood why Paul Merson avoided the spray from the champagne bottles when Portsmouth won promotion. Though there was plenty of drinking during his playing days, Knight's problems came to the surface at the end of his career when restrictions on his consumption were no more. 'They put me through Sporting Chance and that saved my life. It was something which came through word of mouth from another former player, who let me know what the PFA could do.'

Ultimately, the PFA financed Knight's treatment too: 'You have to hit rock bottom and I did to end up looking for their help.' It was several years after his retirement as a player that Knight found himself in trouble from playing, he found himself in trouble. 'I went off the rails. Some invested or did whatever they needed, got a business running which is great, or got into coaching or management and found that made up for that buzz.' Knight had taken on the role of goalkeeping coach for Portsmouth, a specialism which was not common around the turn of the millennium. 'Unfortunately for me, coaching or management never did, I could never replace the adrenaline buzz and I always struggled with the fact that I wouldn't be able to play anymore.'

Compounded by factors in his personal life, it created a perfect storm. 'My first marriage was coming to an end, and I'd moved across into coaching which didn't fill that gap for me. Obviously I was drinking, I was probably a functioning alcoholic if I'm perfectly honest prior to that, but I had structure around my life and I worked the drinking around my professional life, but once that fell away I had no boundaries and no rules so I ended up sitting in pubs all day feeling sorry for myself, getting more depressed. Very soon you start running out of money and the wheels come off massively and you have to try to get things back on track, and thankfully I had enough people around me to help me to do that.'

He reached his jumping-off point one weekend. 'I'd basically moved out of Portsmouth because of the madness of being in town: I could walk in pubs and people would buy me drinks, that was never a problem but it *was* a problem. In the end I just had a meltdown in a pub, I basically started crying and I didn't want to drink. I'd just gone, I can't really explain it any more than that. I just burst into tears, sobbing, and the people I was with were wondering what was up with me, and I told them "That's it, I've had enough, I can't do [it] no more."' He was fed up of the wasted weekends full of the 'what did I do?' type questions that any alcoholic will know well and, though Knight ascribed no blame to anyone, he put his later reliance on alcohol down to his early days as a footballer. The drinking culture was, for a character like him, a slippery slope to something worse.

He had spoken with a former Brighton player about Sporting Chance in the past, but this time he was determined to go through with it. He made the call and spent 28 days there. 'I was in lots of self-pity, I was feeling sorry for myself, depression, and I know it's a cliché but I was hiding in the bottom of a glass. I was in a destructive cycle, suicidal thoughts and the wheels had come off massively. But I went in there and, I've got to be honest, it was the scariest thing I've ever had to do, but as I worked through the process I had a lightbulb moment. Things started to make sense to me as I went through the 12 steps and even in just the first three steps I started to realise just what alcohol and drinking had really become in my life. It had taken over my life and everything revolved around alcohol. I was very lucky and now ten years down the line I have no thought to want to drink again, I really don't want to go back to that ever again and hopefully that will last. It's a day-by-day thing. I have the normal life problems and that doesn't change obviously, but I'm a lot happier than when I had alcohol in my life.'

Knight broke into the first team at Fratton Park as a 17-year-old. What would he advise someone in an academy at that age today? 'I think they have to realise that the chances of actually making it are pretty slim, and to be prepared for that, to be ready to go and have another career and even if they *do* make it, to always have something else to turn to. Do all your education, get a business running if you have the money for that, whether that's in IT or a digger driver, get something else that you can fall back on and have other interests. Be focussed, but there is a fine line to being brainwashed and I think I possibly became too "tunnel-vision". There is more than just football and people might hate me for saying that but there is, and you can do both. You can have another thing on top of football and even better if it is an interest that can help you when you come out of football. And try and enjoy your football,' he said, concluding, 'I don't know if there's as much enjoyment in football as there used to be.'

18.

WHAT HE DOESN'T SEE

'It is a sin for alcohol to touch the lips
of a player' – Arsène Wenger

W HEN Arsène Wenger arrived at Arsenal in 1996, the club had weathered a number of scandals. George Graham's bungs were one thing. Then there was the notorious antics of the Tuesday club and its protagonists' various brushes with the law. It was a club, too, that was not open to rapid changes in outlook or operation, operating with a 'small c' conservatism.

David Dein had pushed Wenger's credentials when Bruce Rioch had been appointed to replace Stewart Houston, but Peter Hill-Wood and the rest of the board were not immediately convinced. They did not think that a foreign manager would have the *cojones* necessary to take on the drinking culture within the club.

'I actually had cold feet about employing a foreigner at that time,' Hill-Wood said in one interview, 'because we had a tricky squad, and one or two of them had personal problems. I wasn't too sure he would understand it. I liked him immediately. I was just nervous and I think some of my colleagues were as well, whether we were ready for a French coach.' Wenger himself later observed, 'Island mentalities are historically mistrustful of foreign influences.'

When he turned up, burgers and chips were cast aside in favour of fish and chicken: light, protein-rich meats. Their favourite apple pies were still permissible but only once the custard component had been removed. It was known by the players as the 'Evian-broccoli' diet. Old habits die hard, and in 2011 Tony Adams confessed, 'Diet won't change anything if you don't have great players, and I still ate fish and chips every week for the last six years under Arsène Wenger.' Yet the man whose methods had been met with bemusement when he arrived is credited with dragging English football kicking and screaming into a healthier place. The run-till-you-drop mentality fostered under Rioch, Graham and their predecessors was swapped for smart conditioning and expertise.

His wholemeal approach had partly been forged during his time as manager of Nagoya Grampus Eight in Japan. 'The whole way of life there is linked to health,' he told *The Guardian*. 'Their diet is basically boiled vegetables, fish and rice. No fat, no sugar ... I think in England you eat too much sugar and meat and not enough vegetables.' Wenger even mostly eschewed the post-match tipple with the opposition manager that had hitherto been a regular occurrence in the English game. Alex Ferguson once called him 'aloof': 'He's the only manager in the Premiership not to do so,' Ferguson said. 'It would be good for him to accept the tradition.'

There may have been good reason for his reticence where alcohol was concerned. In 2009 Wenger told delegates at a conference that it was because he had grown up living above a pub. His parents owned an establishment by the name of La Croix d'Or in Duttlenheim, Alsace. In the course of his childhood, then, Wenger had first-hand experience of overindulgence. 'There is no better psychological education than growing up in a pub,' he said, 'because when you are five or six years old, you meet all different people and hear how cruel they can be to each other. From an early age you get a practical, psychological education to get into the minds of people.'

It would become a plank of his grand footballing philosophy 'that drink ought not to touch the lips of a player'. He continued, 'The most important thing in our job is to understand what's important in life … If you don't understand how to live at 20, you are finished.' This mirrored Wenger's assertion that if a player has not mastered the technical aspects of the game by the age of 14 they never would. Elsewhere, he remarked, 'I believe in discipline. But the best discipline is always when a player understands it's in his best interests. Success today relies on discipline on and off the field.' As a result, he maintained that he would not 'ban beer completely, because one pint helps relax people. But I do not want the players drinking 15 beers, because that is bad.'

Wenger's logic was simple: 'A footballer's body is his work, if he then destroys that with bad habits like drinking, it's silly. My players will have to change their social habits.' For someone like him, it was a no-brainer: 'It's silly to work hard the whole week and then spoil it by not preparing properly before the game. You can point out what is wrong. Some players act the wrong way because they are not strong enough to fight temptation. Some act the wrong way just because they don't know what the right way is. As a coach I can teach the players the things they're doing wrong without knowing it.' Sometimes his signings would align with this philosophy. In Robert Pires, signed in 2000, he had a teetotaller. In Emmanuel Petit, signed three years previously, well, not so much. William Gallas, who arrived from Chelsea in 2006, was known for his love of champagne and glasses of whisky and coke.

Some years later, Wenger observed that drinking had decreased at the top level in England because the level of competition has been raised so high. Were they to drink irresponsibly, players would simply not get picked. Even before it had got to that stage, their team-mates would have regulated it. 'When you win a cup or a championship, it's down to very small things,' he said. 'At the top level every player has to know what he can do and what he cannot do … There is a lot of competition inside the club and if you don't compete, you don't play.'

When Wenger arrived, Tony Adams was emerging from his chrysalis while Paul Merson was seen to have a lid on his drinking. Yet the prevailing attitude at Highbury remained the same. John Hartson enjoyed those nights in the mid-90s. 'It was very different. George was a fantastic manager …' the player told the journalist and author John Cross '[but] the players were basically doing what they wanted to do in the afternoons. If they wanted to have a few beers then they could. If they wanted an "all-dayer" then they could.'

Hartson went on to explain: 'Everyone was drinking under George. I thought it was great! On the day that I signed, Merse had just come out of the Priory. I thought I'd missed all of the fun! But it was just a party when I first arrived. If you wanted to go out in the afternoon, there was always someone to go out with.' A change would come with the new broom though. 'Wenger got it through to players that that is not the way to live your life,' Hartson said, adding: 'It's not the way if you want to extend your career. If you look at Bouldy, Ray Parlour and, in particular, Tony Adams, they would have been finished and washed up at 32. They trained hard but they partied hard as well.'

Parlour, as we know, roomed with Adams for ten years after David O'Leary's departure, until Adams's own retirement. He was well-loved by the Highbury crowds, in part because he was perceived as that throwback to a previous era of English football. On the day he might have made his debut for Arsenal under Graham, he reckoned he was going along to be an unused substitute. When David Hillier had become injured in the warm-up, Stewart Houston entered the players' lounge to discover that Parlour had consumed three pints with unselected members of the squad. Holding a fourth pint in his hand when Houston found him, his potential debut was snuffed out. Yet even Parlour, when he eventually reached the first team as a young man not unaccustomed to several pints, was surprised by the sheer level of consumption by his team-mates.

The Wenger regime meant that even after Parlour's man-of-the-match performance against Chelsea in the

2002 FA Cup Final, a beer was not going to be officially sanctioned. They had another big game four days later against Manchester United in the league. Parlour tells this story in his autobiography, recalling how he tried to imbibe on the sly with his family at the back of the plane when they returned from Cardiff (where finals were held while Wembley was redeveloped). Wenger, becoming aware of this plan, told him, 'If I see you drinking, that's a fine of a week's wages.' Parlour was not willing to sacrifice £30,000 for one beer. Not yet, anyway. He ended up having a drink when the flight landed and got through ten pints of Guinness the next day. After Arsenal had secured the double through victory over United that Wednesday, Wenger is said to have told Parlour, 'You were superb, Ray. Do you know what it was that made the difference?' Parlour asked him what it was. 'I stopped you drinking that beer on the plane.'

These rules were all part of a broader wave of Wengerian influence. What were then viewed as quirky foreign beliefs would go on to revolutionise the English game. He was appalled by the club's basic training facilities, shared with University College London. At his insistence, and after a fire which hastened their departure, Arsenal moved to a state-of-the-art development at London Colney at the cost of £12 million, which was financed by the sale of Nicolas Anelka in 1999. By any measure, this was light years ahead of their previous facilities, and included ten pitches, a steam room and a hydrotherapy pool. Gone was the ketchup from the canteen, while broccoli was an unwelcome addition to practically every meal served there. The eating competitions on the coach back from away matches were, of course, another casualty. During one journey Steve Bould had reputedly consumed nine full meals while returning from a fixture against Newcastle. That would not be happening again.

Another rule concerned mobile phones. Wenger had grown tired of them trilling away while he was delivering team talks and announced, in all seriousness, that the next time one went off it would incur a £10,000 fine. Sure enough, a few days later there was another meeting and another ringtone chirruped away. It kept ringing. Eventually, Wenger went to his bag. It was his own. 'That's a £10,000 fine for me!' he exclaimed.

Even non-alcoholic liquids had a suspicious French eye cast over them, as Nigel Winterburn was to find out: 'Rehydration was so different: Drinking water,' he said. 'Until 6.30pm after games, the players' lounge was alcohol free. That was important to him – refuelling straight after games … He'd like to travel on the train. He'd look down the carriage and see what you were doing. You'd have to be sure before having a cup of tea – but no sugar.' There would be attempts to circumvent these strictures, however: 'When we were waiting on the platform for a train and he wasn't looking we'd pile into the kiosk and get bags of crisps. I'm sure he knew exactly what was going on but we were performing for him.' Wenger was, of course, aware of it, 'But you have to accept you cannot control the players everywhere,' he said.

Upon arrival at away destinations, there was another new rule: room service was banned. Stephen Hughes remembered how this was enforced: '[Wenger] pulled us all together and told us to stop room service and then stopped the hotel from giving us any extras. He'd tell the hotel to tell him and he'd pull whoever and say: "Why did you try to order room service and a pint of Fanta?"' Sugar and milk in hot drinks were strictly *verboten* too, as Winterburn noted. Adding them to hot drinks was seen by the new manager as a 'disgustingly English habit'. Though he would relent slightly as the years passed as long as the sugar was evenly distributed about the mug, it remained one of his major gripes. 'What's really dreadful is the diet in Britain,' he said. 'The whole day you drink tea with milk and coffee with milk and cakes. If you had a fantasy world of what you shouldn't eat in sport, it's what you eat here.'

Even carbonated water did not escape Wenger's regulation. He believed that the fizz would restrict his players' oxygen intake. In times past, players would have eaten at home before home games, but this was quickly changed too. Instead, they met up for a manager-approved meal before the game and, latterly, even stayed in a hotel the night before home fixtures. Gone too were the Jelly Babies in the dressing room that had been a staple of the Bruce Rioch era. 'I changed a few habits,' Wenger said, 'which isn't easy in a team where the average age is 30 years. At the first match the players were chanting, "We want our Mars bars back!"'. At half-time that day, the players had been quiet and the Frenchman had wondered why, only to be told by Gary Lewin that it was because they were hungry due to the denial of their regular snack.

This continental influence, in its Wengerian guise at least, also saw a change in attitudes to dealing with players on an interpersonal level: if the team had performed badly or lost, there was no incandescent rage, just a few quiet words – 'You know what went wrong' – and a reasoned assessment of the video evidence a day or two later without recourse to ranting or screaming. Infamously, he always refrained from criticising his players in public.

For Arsenal, then, the era of big drinking was firmly over. Some new arrivals, like Dennis Bergkamp, had struggled to understand its prominence in the first place. 'It was something I just couldn't understand,' he said. 'Pre-season, we went to a training camp in Sweden and trained twice a day. In the evening, I went for a walk with my wife and saw all the Arsenal players sitting outside a pub. I thought it was unbelievable. The funny thing is you never noticed it in training because they were so strong and they always gave 100 per cent. I didn't drink, and they respected me. They did, and I thought, "It's part of England, so you've got to respect that."'

Pre-season training camps of the type mentioned by Bergkamp were shaken up too. Drinking was now considered a treat rather than an expectation. Ray Parlour describes how they 'worked their socks off', and at the end of the trip, 'Wenger said we could all go out. We went straight down to the pub and the French lads went to the coffee shop.' Parlour wrote, 'I'll always remember the moment Steve Bould went up to the bar and ordered 35 pints for five of us. After we left the bar, we spotted all the French lads in the coffee shop and they were sitting around smoking. I thought, "How are we going to win the league this year? We're all drunk and they're all smoking." We ended up winning the double.'

During that trip to Austria, one French player, Gilles Grimandi, had requested a night out with the English players. When that order of 35 pints was made for five players at 6.30pm that evening, he asked 'who else is coming?' Grimandi had settled for a solitary small glass of wine. That level of drinking would not be feasible two decades later. 'The physical constraints have massively changed,' Wenger explained. 'The players 20 years ago were as much winners as today. They had more freedom than today because the physical demands are much higher, and because the spying facilities of society have increased. Therefore, it is much more difficult today to be anonymous. On that front the pressure on the players is much bigger than it was during Ray Parlour's time.'

The team's French playing contingent, despite its fondness for the Gauloises and Gitanes, would be another way in which English football was changed. Emmanuel Petit, Thierry Henry and Patrick Vieira were a shift away from the Anglo-Saxon monopoly on the dressing room, diluting the influence of the boozy British core. By 2000, Frenchmen in the squad outnumbered their English counterparts and, discounting two dead rubbers, Arsenal fielded at least one of the 23 Frenchmen signed during this time in every line-up for 15 years after Wenger's arrival.

Just how *English* England's professional leagues were until the 1990s should not be underestimated. The first Arsenal line-up Arsène Wenger named contained no less than nine England internationals (with one more on the bench), plus a Wales international and just one overseas player. The overseas player rule was particularly onerous for clubs across the United Kingdom, since a Scottish player – being from a separate FIFA nation – would be counted as a foreigner. Each team could only have three such foreign players until the framework began to crumble when the Bosman ruling passed the European Court of Justice.

By the time the 1996/97 season arrived, the nationality stipulations that had existed for the previous three decades were gone and the number of foreigners who could be fielded was unrestricted. Before long, teams would field starting 11s containing no Englishmen: Chelsea did so on Boxing Day 1999 under Gianluca Vialli, ending an unbroken 111 years and more than 150,000 games of an Englishman taking the field in a professional capacity in each competitive fixture.

When Arsenal had won the league title in 1989 it was done so without the aid of a single player not born on these islands. A few years later, on the opening weekend of the 1992/93 season, only ten foreigners had taken the field among the 242 players across the 22 Premiership line-ups. Nine seasons after that, less than half of this total was made up of domestically reared players. During the Invincibles season Arsenal had just two English regulars in Sol Campbell and Ashley Cole and in 2005 Wenger named his first all-foreign 15-man squad for a match against Crystal Palace. By 2006 there were none at all. When they faced Real Madrid in a Champions League tie in February of that year, their opponents – with Jonathan Woodgate and David Beckham – had a more English line-up.

Earlier that year, Manchester United had triumphed in the Champions League with eight players who would have been deemed foreigners under the old classification. By 2015, 152 Premier League starting 11s had been without a single British player and not a single side has put out a fully English XI. Players (and their agents) were now powerful.

The Bosman ruling was a profound change that reshaped the contours of European football, but seems to have been harmful for Jean-Marc Bosman as a human being.

✦✦✦

It is to his story which we turn to as this chapter concludes, since the arc of his life's journey – not just his wider impact – are relevant to our interests as well as being part of the reason why Arsène Wenger was able to change the culture of Arsenal football club. In recent years, the Belgian ruefully told one newspaper, 'I'm still waiting for the others to say thank you – Ronaldo, Beckham, all of them.' Observers had predicted chaos for football clubs. The reality, though, was chaos for the man himself. Bosman's victory was a great one for the labour rights and the free movement of those who would follow. His actions, however, had made him toxic within the game. Before long, he had slipped into depression and alcohol abuse which, by the 16th anniversary of the ruling which altered the course of the sport, meant he was facing a personally damning verdict.

Bosman was given a suspended sentence in 2012 for threatening his girlfriend and her daughter, with a court-mandated instruction to sort himself out or face jail time. He had asked Carine, 15, to go and buy him more alcohol, but her mother had refused and the former midfielder had punched her in the face. Earlier that year, he had sat down for a newspaper interview during which he claimed he was 'dry' from alcohol and had been for the previous four years. He sipped wine throughout that conversation.

'All of these Belgian players who went to England, they are earning €300,000 per week, while in my case I'm not earning anything,' he told *The Telegraph* in 2015. He had just had his own state benefits withdrawn by the Belgian government. Before that, there had been a doomed 'Who's The Boz' t-shirt line, merchandise he hoped that players who had benefitted from the ruling would purchase. He sold just one garment, to his agent. The Porsche Carrera and his second house were sold to pay a tax liability.

It had begun in 1990, when Bosman's contract with RFC Liege had expired. The club refused to sell him to Dunkerque – in the second tier of French football – without receiving a transfer fee. He was retained by Liege on far less favourable terms than he had been on originally, but could not join another club. It sounds outrageous, and it was, but this was the reality for footballers across the continent. Nine years later, the ruling which bore his name had made Steve McManaman the highest-paid British player in history when he moved from Liverpool to Real Madrid in a deal thought to be a shade north of £50,000 a week for the Englishman.

That was good for McManaman and thousands of others since. But what about Bosman himself? When the football writer Leander Schaerlaeckens interviewed the Belgian in 2015, Bosman drank Diet Coke which he called 'my new alcohol'. He was then sober just short of a year. Giving up then marked the end of 12 years of sustained drinking. The lasting damage of the case on his mental health, however, is clear. It's all he can talk about, a man who is consumed by the bitterness of the injustice he perceived had been wrought upon him.

19.

LAST ORDERS

'Booze is one of the major evils of the game'
– Bobby Robson

WHAT follows is the tale of two strikers. The first, Jermain Defoe, credits his teetotalism as being a large part of why he had been able to maintain such high standards of fitness (and keep scoring) well into his 30s. So fastidious is he about it that he will ask for a white wine sauce to be cooked *sans* white wine when he's eating out at a restaurant. When he watches *Match of the Day*, it is accompanied by nothing stronger than a cup of green tea, a habit which he attributes to Les Ferdinand.

Defoe's abstemiousness was given an added impetus following the death of his father from throat cancer in 2012. 'I don't drink, because I don't think I need to,' he told *The Independent* a few years later. 'When I finish playing one day, I can say to myself, "I did everything right." That's the time when you can enjoy yourself and, I suppose, drink although I don't think I'll really drink. I don't think I'll want to. I've never said it before, my dad used to drink a lot so that's one of the reasons why I don't.'

Though his reasoning is a combination of both sporting and personal concern, Defoe is part of a growing trend of elite performers who – for the duration of their footballing career, at least – are rigorously sparing in their alcohol consumption. The Liverpool squad which defeated Tottenham in the 2019 Champions League Final is said to contain, according to Jürgen Klopp, just half a dozen drinkers.

'All along,' Defoe continued in conversation with *The Independent,* 'I've tried not to get in that habit of drinking, because you don't need it if you want to keep performing at the highest level for a long time.' He stressed that, while he was no saint, 'I think you get more out of yourself if you don't drink. I'm not saying I don't do anything wrong … But I do try to do the right things. If you look after yourself and you don't drink, you eat the right things, you have rests, you sleep then you feel ready for the game at the weekend and you've given yourself the best chance because you've not gone out drinking.'

This type of attitude might be why players like Wayne Rooney appear like a throwback to a previous age of footballers. When Defoe was giving these interviews in late 2016, Wayne Rooney had just been photographed glassy-eyed at a complete stranger's wedding reception at 5am. It led some pundits to wonder whether Rooney could have made more of his undoubted talent if he'd had the discipline to deny himself at certain moments during his career.

Rooney's indiscretion, such as it was, had come after England's 3-0 win over Scotland in a qualifier the day before. It led to the FA banning players from 'nights out' of any description while on England duty in future. An FA statement read: 'England personnel have a responsibility to behave appropriately at all times. We will be reviewing our policy around free time while on international duty.' Though the players' every waking moment would not be monitored, their time would be divided up into three- or four-hour windows, enough to play a round of golf, for example, but requiring them to show their face at the end. For Rooney, it seemed to symbolise a drift in his personal fortunes. He had become peripheral to both Manchester United and England, having been dropped the previous month ahead of a match with Slovenia. While the narrative around him has scarcely touched on the 'A' word in the same way it has for others, comparisons are often made with contemporaries such as Defoe, as well as his former United team-mate Cristiano Ronaldo, whose ascetic nutritional regime is legendary.

His fellow Englishman Defoe's attitude was not one he adopted in his 30s to eke out a few more precious years from his career. Under Harry Redknapp at Tottenham, the team had organised a Christmas party without their boss's knowledge. Defoe did not badmouth them, but he was not afraid to speak about the reasons for his non-participation. 'If you're someone who goes out drinking, then you'll only go backwards ... how are you meant to improve if you're doing stuff like that?' One previous England international, Stanley Matthews, a teetotal vegetarian, would have approved.

Defoe explained that he agreed with Redknapp's dismay at their actions and questioning of the mentality of his team-mates. 'If someone were to offer me a glass of wine, I'd tell them that I didn't need to do that. I wasn't doing it at the start of the season [2009/10], when everything was working for me, so why do it now? Alcohol is not something I've ever really been around. It starts when you're young, so I've always tried to separate myself from it. Growing up, your friends might drink on the streets and you could get involved in it but I've always been away from that.'

It was said that Rooney had been 'stumbling around' and 'could not string a sentence together' as he posed for photographs that night on England duty in 2016, partying with wedding guests and tinkling the ivories into the wee small hours. Yet Rooney and his entourage would go on to brand the situation as 'disgraceful', arguing that the media were not showing him enough respect. 'It feels as if the media are trying to write my obituary and I won't let that happen,' a statement from his camp read. Less than a year later, Rooney was arrested for drink-driving after being caught three times over the legal limit at two in the morning. It was, he said, a 'terrible mistake'. An Everton player by now, the club fined him two weeks' wages, which amounted to a reported £300,000. The court sentenced him to 100 hours of community service. It had happened during an international break, where his services were no longer required.

Footballers in the 'Rooney' mould are ones that had largely vanished from the English game by the turn of the millennium, an unabashed boozer of the Bryan Robson disposition. The so-called 'golden generation' of Frank Lampard, Steven Gerrard, Paul Scholes, were hardly renowned as raconteurs or party boys – save for a few youthful indiscretions – but as singularly driven, model professionals. Yet Rooney was arrested again a little over a year later at Dulles airport in Virginia, during the week before Christmas 2018. Now turning out for DC United aged 33, he had drunk several beers and apparently taken a few sleeping pills on a flight back from Saudi Arabia. When his plane landed, he had then gone to an airport bar to watch Manchester United play Liverpool in what transpired to be Jose Mourinho's last game in charge at Old Trafford. In the event, he was fined $25 and ordered to pay $91 in costs but some went as far as to suggest that he was criminalised for being English. His crime had been to yell 'fucking c--t' at a TV screen as Liverpool cruised to victory, and it is perhaps fair to say that it would have been unremarkable on these shores.

Where Cristiano Ronaldo – and, recently signed by Rangers at the age of 36, Defoe – have been able to continue a top-level career, Rooney's has tailed off much sooner. Their birthdays just eight months apart, Rooney is still a great player by MLS standards, yet Ronaldo has recently commanded a transfer fee in excess of €100 million when he was sold to Juventus. Assiduously avoiding anything sweet – including, for the most part, alcohol – he often boasts of having the bodily age of a 27-year-old. Rooney, on the other hand, is clearly partial to a beer or two and fond of the odd cigarette. Could he have had a longer career with United? There is surely a genetic element involved in the differences between one footballer and another, but every small sacrifice that Ronaldo has made is likely to have prolonged his viability as an elite athlete. Each of Rooney's moments of weakness will have shortened his.

Seen within a wider context, the retirement age for professional footballers has shifted upwards as advances have been made in understanding conditioning, preparation and diet. Where once players might have burst onto the scene before their 18th birthday, increasingly these are rarities as the necessity of stronger players has become the norm. Top-level careers have tended to properly start at a later age – perhaps 21 or 22, as has long been the case in Italy – meaning that retirement will often be deferred to a commensurately later age. Though Major League Soccer should not be seen as a retirement home, Rooney was essentially a busted flush in a European context by his late 20s, while those around him were pushing into their prime years.

Though tabloid tales and lurid autobiographies may have given the impression otherwise, the process of English football's sobering up had already begun in the 1990s. The 'dentist's chair' side of Euro 96 probably drank less than all England tournament squads that had gone before it, including the victors in 1966. Stan Bowles, who played five times for England in the mid-70s in his own boozy heyday, was similarly clear. 'It seems the media are promoting these exclusives as if this sort of behaviour is new to the game,' he wrote in his autobiography. 'I can assure you that is certainly not the case, it was even worse in the 70s.' Paul Merson believes that it is simply because indiscretions were easier to capture. 'The drinking is no worse than before but the focus is bigger,' he wrote in his most recent autobiography. 'When we were winning trophies at Arsenal we used to go out every Tuesday without fail ... it was never in the papers. Nowadays you could be playing for the worst team in the world and still get the headlines if you are caught drinking …'

❧❧❧

It was on 6 August 1996 – 41 days after England's Euro 96 exit – that Alan Shearer returned home, signing for Newcastle United. The Scottish and Newcastle brewery gave its 1,500 workers the afternoon off. Yet in 2019, it barely seems conceivable that clubs operating at this level could sustain this arrangement. Quite simply, breweries – who had for so long underwritten many of England's most prestigious football clubs – no longer play the role in the game that they did even 25 years ago. Shirt sponsorships have shifted from alcohol firms – albeit fleetingly to betting businesses as football begins to reckon with its gambling problem – and now beyond as these vices are discarded in an era where football seeks to present a scrubbed-up image to its global audience. Indeed, no better illustration than domestic treble-winning Manchester City are now partly owned by a gulf state within which alcohol consumption is officially prohibited.

As football's relationship with drink has moderated, the way England as a nation drinks has changed too. When Tony Blair's 'Cool Britannia' government arrived in 1997, the time was seen as ripe for a further loosening of regulations, especially around opening hours. Going home at 11pm was hardly trendy or continental. Ahead of the 2001 general election, the Labour party sent a pre-poll text message reading 'cdnt give a? xxxx 4 lst orders? Thn vote Lbr on thrsday 4 xtra time.' After winning that election, they legislated for such a change, which became fully operational in 2005. Now any pub could theoretically stay open beyond 11pm, and most did. Some establishments were permitted to open until 2am on certain nights, and by 2003 61 per cent were doing so. Many city centres that had been run down, shabby affairs in the late 1980s were – at least on the surface – rejuvenated by this infusion of cash and youthful energy.

For a number of these outlets, football was a handy marketing vehicle to draw young men into their orbit. Where for decades pubs had been the base that a Sunday league team might have for its post-match debriefing sessions in return for some sponsorship money, now the pub was a place to go and watch a top-level match on Sky Sports, a luxury too expensive for the homes of many young fans, both then and now.

In the years following the dawning of a new millennium, levels of alcohol consumption were rising fast, with binge drinking among the young a significant contributor. A third of 20-something men were classed as such, where 'binging' was defined as drinking twice the daily recommended amount (nine units) in one sitting. Others used five or more drinks as a measure, but by any calculation England sat near the top of the table. The harms associated with alcohol were costing the economy £20 billion annually and the demon drink was responsible for half of all violent crime, including 360,000 incidences of domestic violence in a single year. Meanwhile, up to 1,000 suicides per year attributed alcohol as a factor. Though the drinks market was valued at £30 billion within the wider economy, its tax revenue was only bringing £7 billion into treasury coffers. Crucially, however, it employed one million people in one way or another, making it a tricky target for legislators.

Nevertheless, it was urged from many disparate quarters that levels of consumption per person should be reduced to 1970s levels. In 2004 Tony Blair wondered if binge drinking was a 'new British disease'. Thirty-one per cent of the population said they had drunk twice as much or more than the 'recommended daily allowance' in the previous week, putting them well within the parameters of 'harmful' drinking. Much of this drinking was being done at home (often before heading out to a pub or club later in the evening). So much so, in fact, that in-pub drinking had decreased slightly. Largely down to the tax freezes and economies of scale that supermarkets enjoyed, alcohol was 65 per cent more affordable in 2001 than it had been 20 years earlier.

When opening hours were relaxed in 2005, its effect was to shift peak violence in town and city centres, drifting from just after 11pm to 3am. Consumption, though falling slightly, was 26 per cent higher in 2004 than it had been in 1974. Alcohol-related mortality had doubled. Cases of liver cirrhosis had risen 95 per cent between the years 2000 and 2007 and hospital admissions associated with drinking soared by a third in a similar timeframe. Perhaps as a result, a few short years later, in 2008, a widespread change in attitudes had taken place: Cool Britannia had been discarded in favour of Brownite prudence and his chancellor, Alistair Darling, put alcohol taxes up for the first time in ten years.

That same year, Paul Merson was forced to move back into his parents' ex-council house in St Albans after defaulting on his mortgage payments as a result of his gambling. In *How Not To Be A Professional Footballer*, published in 2011, he wrote of how he had also 'fallen off several wagons'. The most common stories we tend to hear are from those footballers who have – at that point in time – 'beaten their demons' or at least give the appearance of having done so. Their biographies will contain a familiar narrative arc which culminates with their seeking help, receiving it and coming out the other side of some turbulent years.

In the weeks of spring 2019 during which I have concluded the final passages of this book, Paul Merson has returned to meetings of Alcoholics Anonymous and Gamblers Anonymous. As he once said, 'The game isn't over until the final whistle blows.'

BIBLIOGRAPHY

Books

Alcoholics Anonymous World Service *Twelve Steps and Twelve Traditions* (AA World Services, 2013)

Adams, Tony, *Addicted* (Willow, 1999)

Adams, Tony *Sober: Football. My Story. My Life.* (Simon & Schuster, 2018)

Atkins, Fred *Arsenal: The French Connection* (CreateSpace, 2016)

Atkinson, Ron *The Manager* (deCoubertin Books, 2016)

Bailey, Peter *Leisure and Class in Victorian England: Rational Recreation and the Contest for Control* (Routledge, 1987)

Barton, Joey *No Nonsense: The Autobiography* (Simon & Schuster, 2016)

Beaven, Brad *Leisure, citizenship and working class men in Britain, 1850-1945* (Manchester University Press, 2009)

Belton, Brian *Red Dawn Manchester United The Early Years* (Endeavour Media, 2013)

Belton, Brian *The Thames Ironworks: A History of East London Industrial and Sporting Heritage* (The History Press, 2015)

Best, George *Blessed - The Autobiography* (Ebury, 2012)

Bowles, Stan *Stan Bowles: The Autobiography* (Orion, 2005)

Broughton, Drewe *And Then What...?* (Drewe Broughton Media, 2018)

Carlisle, Clarke *You Don't Know Me, But . . .: A Footballer's Life* (Simon & Schuster, 2013)

Clough, Brian *Clough The Autobiography* (Transworld Digital, 2009)

Clough, Brian *Cloughie: Walking on Water* (Headline, 2014)

Collins, Tony and Vamplew, Wray *Mud, Sweat and Beers: A Cultural History of Sport and Alcohol* (Berg 3PL, 2002)

Conn, David *The Football Business: The Modern Football Classic* (Mainstream Publishing, 2002)

Crerand, Paddy *Paddy Crerand: Never Turn the Other Cheek* (HarperSport, 2014)

Cross, John *Arsène Wenger: The Inside Story of Arsenal Under Wenger* (Simon & Schuster, 2018)

Doherty, Peter *Spotlight on Football* (Art & Educational Publishers, 1948)

Ferguson, Alex *Alex Ferguson: 6 Years at United* (Mainstream, 2013)

Ferguson, Alex *Alex Ferguson My Autobiography* (Hodder, 2014)

Ferguson, Alex *Managing My Life: My Autobiography* (Hodder & Stoughton, 2011)

Forsyth, Mark *A Short History of Drunkenness* (Penguin, 2017)

Francis, Charles *History of Blackburn Rovers Football Club 1875-1925 (Classic Reprint)* (Soccer Books Ltd, 2005)

Gascoigne, Paul *Gazza: My Story* (Headline, 2014)

Gately, Iain *Drink: A Cultural History of Alcohol* (Avery, 2009)

Gernon, Alan *Retired: What Happens to Footballers When the Game's Up* (Pitch Publishing, 2016)

Gibbons, Michael *When Football Came Home: England, the English and Euro 96* (Pitch Publishing, 2016)

Gogarty, Paul and Williamson, Ian *Winning at all Costs: Sporting Gods and Their Demons* (JR Books, 2009)

Goulding, Jeff *Red Odyssey: Liverpool FC 1892-2017* (Pitch Publishing, 2018)

Greaves, Jimmy *Greavsie: The Autobiography* (Sphere, 2009)

Greaves, Jimmy *This One's On Me* (Arthur Barker, 1979)

Hamilton, Duncan *Immortal* (Cornerstone, 2013)

Hamilton, Duncan *Provided You Don't Kiss Me: 20 Years with Brian Clough* (Harper Perennial, 2008)

Harding, John and Taylor, Gordon *Living To Play: From Soccer Slaves to Socceratti - A Social History of the Professionals* (Robson Books, 2003)

Harris, Nick *The Foreign Revolution: How Overseas Footballers Changed the English Game* (Aurum Press, 2006)

Hughes, Simon *Red Machine: Liverpool FC in the '80s: The Players' Stories* (Mainstream, 2014)

Inglis, Simon *League Football and the Men Who Made it* (HarperCollinsWillow, 1988)

James, Gary *Manchester The City Years 1857-2012* (James Ward, 2014)

Joannou, Paul *The Hughie Gallacher Story* (Breedon Books, 1989)

King, Martin, Knight, Martin and Osgood Peter *Ossie: King of Stamford Bridge* (Mainstream Sport, 2012)

Knight, Alan and Farmery, Colin *Legend: The Alan Knight Story* (Legendary Publishing, 2003)

Lovejoy, Joe and Best, George *Bestie: A Portrait of A Legend* (Sidgwick & Jackson, 2012)

Macdonald, Malcolm and Malam, Colin *Supermac: My Autobiography* (Highdown, 2004)

McGrath, Paul *Back from the Brink: The Autobiography* (Cornerstone, 2010)

McGuigan, Paul and Hewitt, Paolo *The Greatest Footballer You Never Saw: The Robin Friday Story* (Mainstream, 2011)

Merson, Paul *Hero and Villain* (Willow, 2000)

Merson, Paul *How Not to Be a Professional Footballer* (HarperSport, 2011)

Merson, Paul *Rock Bottom* (Bloomsbury, 1996)

Mitten, Andy *We're the Famous Man United: Old Trafford in the Eighties: The Players' Stories* (Vision Sports Publishing, 2015)

Morris, Terry *Vain Games of No Value?: A Social History of Association Football in Britain During Its First Long Century* (AuthorHouse, 2016)

MUFC *The Official Illustrated History of Manchester United 1878-2010* (Simon & Schuster, 2010)

Nevin, Pat and Sik, George *In Ma Head, Son!: Footballer's Mind Revealed* (Headline, 1998)

Nicholls, James *The politics of alcohol* (Manchester University Press, 2013)

Parlour, Ray *The Romford Pelé: It's only Ray Parlour's autobiography* (Cornerstone Digital, 2016)

Rippon, Anton *The Aston Villa Story* (Breedon Books, 1993)

Roberts, Christian *Life Is A Game of Inches* (Vertical Editions, 2010)

Robson, Bryan *Robbo - My Autobiography* (Hodder & Stoughton, 2012)

Roderick, Martin *The Work of Professional Football: A Labour of Love?* (Routledge, 2006)

Sanders, Richard *Beastly Fury: The Strange Birth of British Football* (Transworld, 2010)

Sansom, Kenny *To Cap It All* (John Blake, 2010)

Spurling, Jon *Rebels for the Cause: The Alternative History of Arsenal Football Club* (Mainstream, 2012)

Spurling, Jon *Highbury: The Story of Arsenal in N.5* (Orion, 2010)

Spurling, Jon *Top Guns: Arsenal in the 1990s* (Aureus Publishing, 2017)

Stainback, Robert *Alcohol and Sport* (Human Kinetics, Europe, 1997)

Taw, Thomas *Football's Twelve Apostles: The Making of the League 1886-1889* (Desert Island eBooks, 2012)

Taylor, Daniel and Owen, Jonny *I Believe In Miracles: The Remarkable Story of Brian Clough's European Cup-winning Team* (Headline, 2015)

Taylor, Matthew *Leaguers: The Making of Professional Football in England: 1900-1939,* (The Chicago University Press, 2007)

Taylor, Peter *With Clough, By Taylor* (Biteback Publishing, 2019)

Tongue, Steve *Turf Wars* (Pitch Publishing, 2018)

Vaillant, George *The Natural History of Alcoholism Revisited* (Harvard University Press, 1995)

Walvin, James *The People's Game: The History of Football Revisited* (Mainstream Sport, 2014)

Wenner, Lawrence (ed.) *Fallen Sport Heroes, Media, Celebrity Culture* (Peter Lang Publishing, 2013)

White, Jim *Manchester United: The Biography* (Sphere, 2010)

Whiteside, Norman *Determined: The Autobiography* (Headline, 2014)

Wilson, Alan *Team of all the Macs* (Vertical Editions, 2011)

Wilson, Jonathan *Brian Clough: Nobody Ever Says Thank You* (Orion, 2011)

Winner, David *Those Feet: A Sensual History of English Football* (Bloomsbury, 2006)

Winter, Henry *Fifty Years of Hurt: The Story of England Football and Why We Never Stop Believing* (Transworld, 2016)

Journal articles

Borkman, Thomasina *The Twelve-Step Recovery Model of AA: A Voluntary Mutual Help Association* (Recent Developments in Alcoholism, 2008)

Coakley, Jay *Leaving Competitive Sport: Retirement or Rebirth?* (National Association for Physical Education in Higher Education, 1983)

Collins, Tony and Vamplew, Wray *The Pub, the Drinks Trade and the Early Years of Modern Football* (Sports Historian, 2000)

Gouttebarge, Vincent, Aoki, Haruhito and Kerkhoffs, Gino *Prevalence and determinants of symptoms related to mental disorders in retired male professional footballers* (The Journal of Sports Medicine and Physical Fitness, 2015)

Jones, Carwyn *Alcoholism and recovery: A case study of a former professional footballer* (International Review for the Sociology of Sport, 2013)

Lakasing, Edin and Mirza, Zul *Football and alcohol: a short diary of a long and complex relationship* (London Journal of Primary Care, 2009)

Rafalovich, Adam *Keep Coming Back! Narcotics Anonymous narrative and recovering-addict identity* (Contemporary Drug Problems, 1999)